Lewis David

Emotions: Overcome Stress, Anxiety & Negativity in 10 Days

WinsPress.com

Text Copyright © Lewis David Wins Press 2020

All rights reserved. No part of this publication may be reproduced, or transmitted in any form or by any means, electronic or otherwise, without written permission from the author.

Legal & Disclaimer

The information contained in this book is not designed to replace or take the place of any form of medicine or professional medical advice. The information contained in this book has been compiled from sources deemed reliable, and it is accurate to the best of the Author's knowledge; however, the Author cannot guarantee its accuracy and validity and cannot be held liable for any errors or omissions. Changes are periodically made to this book. You must consult your doctor or get professional medical advice before using any of the suggested remedies, techniques, or information in this book. Upon using the information contained in this book, you agree to hold harmless the Author from and against any damages, costs, and expenses, including any legal fees potentially resulting from the application of any of the information provided by this guide.

This disclaimer applies to any damages or injury caused by the use and application, whether directly or indirectly, of any advice or information presented, whether for breach of contract, tort, negligence, personal injury, criminal intent, or under any other cause of action. You agree to accept all risks of using the information presented inside this book. You need to consult a professional medical practitioner before embarking on any program or information in this book.

About the Author.

Lewis David is a therapist and trainer, specializing in behavioural and emotional issues. He has worked with thousands of clients in government-funded services and private practice in England.

He began writing about his work in 2017 and, with two Amazon bestsellers behind him, now concentrates on his writing.

By the Same Author

Change Your Life Today

The 10-Day Alcohol Detox Plan

For more information on these books, visit:
winspress.com

Contents

About the Author. 4

Getting Started. 7

Day One. 17

In Two Minds. 19

Emotional Conditions. 27

Deep Relaxation. 37

Day Two. 43

Thoughts. 45

The Rule of Three. 51

Dynamic De-stress. 61

Day Three. 67

The Scale of Ten. 68

What If? 77

Day Four. 85

Active Awareness. 87

The Kiwi Vine. 97

Clouds. 103

Day Five. 111

Approval. 113

Assumptions. 123

Day Six. 129

Anger. 131

Resentment. 141

Day Seven.. 149
Addictive Behaviours. 151
The Habits Audit... 163
Day Eight.. 169
Negativity... 171
Procrastination. 179
Day Nine. 187
Action... 189
Hypnotherapy. 199
Day Ten. 205
The Process. 207
After Day 10. 217
Extra Resources 221
Emotional Attachment... 222
Don't Wait Until You're Ready. 233
Thank You.. 241

Getting Started.

The subtitle of this book makes a bold statement of intent: overcome anxiety, stress and negativity. To do that, you will need to do a little more than just read this book. You need to absorb its suggestions and apply the ideas as you go along. For this reason, I have laid this book out for you to read over 10 days.

I have run many 10-day programs working in public health. These were face-to-face group workshops I created for a range of emotional and behavioural needs. To evidence the effectiveness of the programs, the clients filled out self-assessment health and wellness questionnaires before and after the course, so we could measure the difference the workshops had made. The results were impressive.

I was, however, somewhat concerned about whether the 10-day format would work in the form of a self-study book. As it turns out, it works wonderfully well. I released my first book in this format last year, "The 10-Day Alcohol Detox Plan", a book intended for people wanting a break from drinking. The feedback has been amazing. Within weeks, the book became an Amazon #1 Bestseller in its category in both the United States and the United Kingdom. It has changed people's lives in just 10 days. I'm confident the same will happen for emotional issues as well.

You could sit down and read this whole of this book in a day. But research shows that if you do that, you will remember barely 10%. Think about the books you read last year. Can you remember everything in them? Can you even remember the names of all the books you read last year? So if you want to get the full benefit from this book, you will need to do more than just give it a quick read.

If you want to read this book as fast as possible, then you are thinking like a stressed person and I want you to move on from that painful way of thinking. What you are reading is important. Give it time.

When you have read the section for the day, I want you to consider what you have read and apply it to your day. I will indicate as we go along where I want you to try out something you have read. I recommend that you try everything, rather than choosing the concepts that appeal to you. Everything in this book has worked for other people, so why not for you? If you miss out parts of the book, you will miss ways to transform your life for the better.

Look for opportunities to use what you have learned. In this way, you will not only read the book, but you will also live it. As a result, you will give your new knowledge a chance to sink in properly and reprogram your subconscious with positive new ways of managing your emotions.

Reading this book daily will not take up a lot of time, so even if you are busy, you can fit it into your day. If you really want to read the whole thing before you do the 10 days, that's okay, but go back over the material daily afterwards. It would be best to do the 10 days on consecutive days if you can, to keep up the momentum. But if a particular strategy needs more time than one day for you, by all means, take another day or two to get used to using it, rather than rushing it. But avoid having days off from the book. It's easy work - this is a book to enjoy.

There are no long, written exercises, nothing is a drudge. You will need a notepad a few times, but that's all. You might have read books on a similar subject to this that have workbooks for you to fill out. There isn't one here. This is a life book. Mainly, you need to read the text for the day, then try out what you have learned. On some days, there are also complimentary recordings for you to listen to.

I have written this book in a way that you can easily dip into it as a reference work after you have done the 10 days. Although the chapters follow a sequence, you can read each chapter as a stand-alone essay on its own theme. In this way, the book will be simple for you to come back to and reassess any part of it. I hope that is helpful.

Some concepts here have never appeared in print before. They have evolved over thousands of hours of interaction between my clients and me. I am sharing those concepts now because they work.

After the 10 days, you will have the skills to overcome the typical emotionally challenging situations that crop up in our lives. You will not eliminate your emotions, and neither should you try, as they are a part of being human. But you will know how to stop them getting out of hand.

Take fear, for example. This would seem to most people to be a negative emotion. However, everyone experiences fear. The bravest person you ever met experiences fear. If we did not have the emotion of fear, we would not understand caution and would place ourselves in danger. Without fear, humanity would not have survived until now. Predators would have eaten our ancestors long ago. Fear has a vital role to play in our lives. Some people put themselves in scary situations for fun, like riding a rollercoaster or skydiving – fear and excitement are similar feelings.

But if fear runs your life, if it makes it difficult for you to do the normal things people do, then you need ways to overcome it and live a happier life.

Another emotion that people want to avoid is sadness. We would all prefer to feel happy. However, sadness has a role to play in our wellbeing. If you experience a loss in your life, as we all inevitably do from time to time, experiencing sadness is not only normal, it is the start of the healing process that will eventually bring you back to a happier way of thinking.

But if you feel sad for no reason, or if you dwell on the pain of past events, then you need ways of keeping this emotion in balance.

Even anger can have a positive side. When injustice enters our lives, it's normal to feel angry, and letting some anger out to have its moment is the starting point of a return to balance, as long as you stay within safe boundaries, so you will not hurt yourself or anyone else – go ahead and punch your pillow.

But if your anger spills over into uncontrolled raging, or if anger is your default reaction to the annoyances of daily life, robbing you of contentment in your world, then you need ways to defuse it, or peace of mind will constantly elude you.

However, while some apparently undesirable feelings have a beneficial side, many emotions just seem to bring us distress and hurt without doing us any good. They are toxic, and there are many of them: self-pity, outrage, hate, despair, guilt, shame, resentment, panic, jealousy, greed, negativity, bitterness, humiliation – they cause havoc wherever they go.

They are like pain-birds flying into our lives, bringing anxiety, stress, and anguish.

While negative feelings are inevitable, there is no need for them to spoil your life. You will learn how to overcome these emotions quickly when they turn up, and even how to stop them before they begin.

This book is solution-focused, so although I will discuss how we experience emotional pain, stress, anxiety and negativity, I will not be going into detail. Why not? Well, if you have any of these problems, you know what they are like already. You don't need me to tell you how you feel. You are the world's number one expert on how you feel. You want to know how to feel *better*, and this book does that in abundance.

I will discuss insights that you might not have found in other books. I will write in language that will make tricky subjects easy to understand, so you can go straight to the good stuff without having to wade through pages of techno-babble. My ambition is that you will find this book enjoyable and informative.

Making life changes doesn't have to be hard work. It can be fun. It can be a game. If that sounds crazy, consider how much you learned when you were a child from having fun and playing games. This is how we grow. A small child regards playing in a school sand pit as fun. A teacher will see that as learning. So I encourage you to spend some time and play with the concepts you find in these pages.

As the emotional issues in the book are all related to each other, you will find that key themes crop up several times throughout the book. This will help you grasp the concepts naturally, without feeling as though you are studying a dry textbook. New ideas take root in our minds after we see them several times and from different angles.

You can look at your problems as often and for as long as you like and it won't change a thing. You already know what your emotional issues are. Although you might think focusing on your problems will help, which is probably what you have been doing, it will not, it will just drag your mood lower. Focusing on solutions changes everything. This book will guide you to the solutions. I cannot be sure exactly which part of this book will have the greatest impact on your life, which is why it's important to try all the ideas in this book. To help, I have drawn on several therapies:

- Cognitive Therapy, to help you identify where your thinking is causing emotional pain and how to turn that around.
- Solution-Focused Thinking, to show you how simple strategies will give you effortless momentum to change key aspects of your life.
- Mindfulness, so you can get some peace in your head and enjoy the here-and-now while you make changes.
- Deep Relaxation, to bring you instant relief from stress.
- Hypnotherapy, so you can effortlessly reprogram your subconscious to support you.

As you read through the book, you will find links to audio downloads for Mindful Therapy, Deep Relaxation, and Hypnotherapy that we have specially prepared for you. You just need to listen, relax, and enjoy. I have collaborated with Antonia Ryan to produce the recordings. Antonia is a highly experienced professional with a background of working in education and social care. She graduated from Queens University in Ireland, has qualifications in teaching, psychology and hypnotherapy, and qualified to teach meditation in Glastonbury, England.

At the end of the 10 days, you will have the know-how to handle common emotional issues when they occur. You won't need to wait long to try out your new skills, as these issues crop up all the time. You will also have the skills to help you move on when more dramatic and upsetting events happen. Most people should find this book provides all they need, but if you suspect you need additional face-to-face support, consult your doctor.

It's essential that you don't stop after the 10 days, as you can easily slip back into old, self-defeating ways. I have included an aftercare program for you to follow on from the 10 days. You will discover more about this at the end of the book.

Are you ready for day one?

Day One.

In Two Minds.

When we are undecided, we sometimes say we are in two minds. This is quite an accurate explanation of how things are. In your head, you have a logical mind and an emotional mind.

I mean this literally. Your logical mind is located at the front of your brain. You actively engage with it, so you are aware that you are thinking. As I write this book, my logical mind is fully engaged. If I get stuck about what to write next, I will consciously use my logical mind to find a way forward. It's this part of your brain that sets humans apart from other species because it gives us the abilities to use imagination and solve problems. Where nothing previously existed, we can conceive an idea and then find a way to make it real.

If you look around, you can see the results of our imagination everywhere: the town you live in, the car you drive, the building you call home, the clothes you wear, the furniture you are relaxing on at this very moment. In the past, all these things were no more than someone's vision. A short time ago, this book only existed in my imagination, but now you are reading it. That conscious part of our brain has shaped our world, but it's not the most powerful part of your mind.

Your emotional mind is located farther back in your head. You don't consciously engage with it. Instead, it engages with you and, unlike your logical side, which switches off when you sleep, the emotional mind runs all the time. As soon as you doze off for a second, it takes centre-stage in your dreams. It works on a subconscious level, all the time monitoring your world, processing the information you are constantly collecting through your senses and sending you thoughts and feelings in a never-ending stream.

If you are watching a movie, the way you feel about the characters will change continuously as the plot unfolds and you learn more about them. You might start off disliking a character, but end up loving them after your feelings have gone through all shades of opinion. You don't consciously keep thinking, "Do I like these characters?" You don't need to, because your emotional mind is constantly re-testing the information it receives about them. In the real world also, you are endlessly evaluating how you feel about every person you know. Even your feelings about those you truly love will fluctuate within a range.

It's not just people. Your emotional mind crunches every bit of data your senses bring in, forming instant opinions and then firing them out at you in the form of thoughts and feelings, even while you sleep. Have you ever gone to bed feeling cheerful, only to feel like your world has ended in the morning? Your mood has collapsed overnight for no reason that you know. You go through your morning routine feeling like something awful has happened, although nothing has. Then suddenly, for no obvious reason, your mood lifts. What was that all about? Well, no doubt your emotional mind had changed its ideas about how it interpreted the world while you were asleep but you didn't know until you woke up.

You cannot control the emotional mind in the same way you can your logical side, as it is in charge, subconsciously manipulating your emotional landscape. We try to control it with logic and can have some limited success. But it requires great effort and usually feels like you are holding back a dam that at some point is going to burst, it's just a question of time.

This is why we struggle with willpower. How many times have you decided to change a behaviour to improve yourself, such as going on a diet, only for your willpower to fall apart? You might keep going on willpower for a few days, but if your emotional mind is screaming "Gimme, gimme!" every time you go near the kitchen, your resolve will eventually crumble.

Your emotional mind is too powerful for your logical side, sometimes it seems like comparing the power of a modern computer to an old-fashioned pocket calculator. If you leave it to run the show, as most people do, you can expect your moods to go up and down constantly, stress and anxiety will be with you most of the time, and your feelings will run your life. But if this all sounds all gloom and doom, don't worry. Solutions exist, and they aren't complicated.

Imagine your emotions are being run by a computer at the back of your head. Now, think about this for a moment: you can re-program computers to work as you want, so why not your emotions? Imagine getting the power of your emotions working for you, instead of shoving you around randomly.

Well, you can.

Your emotional mind is reacting to the data it's picking up from your senses. It will be aware of every sound and smell in your environment far more than you are on a conscious level. It will monitor everything you see in great detail at colossal speed. It will pick up on slight changes in temperature, amounts of ambient light, and air movement on your skin. All this information and more is being mashed through and fed back to you as to how it thinks you should feel.

You might expect me to discuss ways of dealing with those feelings, and we will do that in this book. But that's looking at the data (the feelings) that are coming out of your brain. How about taking a step back first and looking at the data that's going in? That's where you can make a difference simply and quickly.

Look at how you are physically right now. Let's start with your temperature. Are you cold, or too hot, or just okay? Are you sitting somewhere comfortably? Is the lighting suitable for reading this book? If not, your emotional brain will dislike the data it's picking up from your senses and it will start sending you feelings that say you are unhappy. It will do this by sending you negative thoughts and shutting off the supply of your brain's natural feel-good chemicals, like dopamine and serotonin (which we will discuss more later).

What you put into your mind via your senses directly affects the feelings you are getting out. If you input negative sensations into your emotional mind, you will get negative feelings coming out.

That is something you can deliberately change.

Classic things to look out for are if you are hungry, angry, lonely or tired. If one of those applies, then take action. Eat if you are hungry, put on some relaxing music if you are angry, call your best friend if you are lonely, or go to bed if you are tired.

Maybe you need a change of environment. If you get out of the space you are in, your senses will be awash with new incoming data for your mind to analyse. If it likes the data it's receiving, it will send you approving thoughts and turn up the supply of the feel-good chemicals in your head.

So next time you feel low for no particular reason, instead of feeling sorry for yourself and getting into a downward spiral, deliberately ask yourself how you can change the data your senses are picking up. Otherwise, you could convince yourself that you are depressed when all you need to do is to turn on the heating, increase the light levels, change the music, or have a snack.

So today, when you have a negative feeling, instead of reacting as you usually do, emotionally, I want you to try something different. Use negative thoughts as an opportunity to learn a new skill. Deliberately engage your logical mind. Try looking at your situation and ask yourself what information your emotional brain is absorbing from your environment via your senses. Is there something it would find objectionable? Think analytically about what you could change then take action.

This will take a certain amount of concentration on your part, or you will immediately react as normal. This is why simply reading this book is insufficient. You need to try the suggestions, or your autopilot will kick in, you will forget what you have read and make no progress.

So I suggest you task yourself with identifying 3 times today when a negative thought or feeling hits you and use the above exercise. It doesn't have to be a dramatically negative emotion. A simple feeling of discomfort is enough to use to get the hang of this way of thinking. What it will show you is that when you have a feeling, you have choices.

A negative thought or feeling is not a command for you to act in a negative way, it is an emotion, and emotions are not commands, they are merely passing events in your mind.

You can act on them if you wish, or you can choose to change the information going into your emotional brain, which will alter the feelings that come out.

Your emotional brain will reward you for feeding it more acceptable data because the good news about that part of your mind is that it gives you all your emotions, not just the toxic ones. It's where your happiness comes from as well. You will have a more contented life if you pay attention to what you feed it.

Most people go through life unaware that they have choices in how they respond to their emotions and that they can deliberately take action to affect the feelings your emotional mind throws out. If you were one of those people, you have just learned a major insight into your inner-self which, on its own, will make a huge difference to your life if you use it. But this is just the start. Let's move on.

Emotional Conditions.

The subtitle of this book refers to three main causes of emotional pain: stress, anxiety and negativity. So what exactly are they?

Stress.

Stress comes from external factors happening in the present. Your emotional mind will respond with a fight-or-flight response. Fight-or-flight is a natural reaction to danger. If you are under physical threat, the emotional brain will tell you either to attack the source of danger or run, depending on the situation, and it decides this in a fraction of a second, far faster than your logical mind can work. This speed could save you. In a life or death situation, you need to react rapidly. If someone aims a gun in your direction, you don't want to hang around while your logical mind assesses the situation; you want to move.

The fight-or-flight response stirs up your hormones and adrenaline in particular. You feel agitated, your heartbeat quickens, and you feel light-headed. In other words, you feel stressed and fearful, which are appropriate responses to physical danger – you need that adrenaline pumping. This is an integral part of our survival instinct which evolved while our ancestors were living in a wild world. Some people still live in a dangerous environment, but for most of us, fight-or-flight is less useful nowadays. If you are at home watching television in your comfortable home in Boston or Bristol, you are unlikely to be attacked by a dangerous animal. Yet you could still experience fear and stress.

This is because your emotional mind will trigger fight-or-flight in response to a threat not only to your body but also to your ego. So you can feel the same stress and fearfulness when threatened with criticism, loss of status, failure, embarrassment or ridicule. Adrenaline will produce similar physical symptoms, even though the pain is emotional. Stressed people feel rushed and unable to enjoy life in the present. They feel there are too many fires to fight in their lives to allow time for relaxation and rewarding activities.

Stress is usually temporary. As soon as whatever is causing the stress passes, so does the stress. If you are having a stressful day at work, for instance, the stress will pass when you leave for home. But stress can also be chronic, in other words, it can be long-term or recurring. So if your job is *always* stressful and you cannot switch off from it when you go home, then that stress will be chronic, at least until you get another job.

External factors only partially account for our stress. We also generate negative emotions from how we think about external stress factors. Take, for example, driving in a busy city. Any driver has external stress in this situation. But what you believe about driving will generate additional internal stress and so will affect your overall stress. If you were a newly qualified driver, your thought might be that it will be frightening, and if that is what you *believe*, that will be how you *feel*. You will be frightened. But another driver might think it will be exciting and will feel exhilaration, rather than fear. A taxi driver will think it will be routine and might feel boredom. So three drivers will experience widely different emotions, depending on what they think, although the external stress - the city traffic - is the same for all three.

We have limited ability to control external stress, as we cannot micromanage everything that happens in the world around us. Trying to control every aspect of your world will leave you exhausted and even more stressed. But, as we will discuss through this book, we can manage how we think about stressful situations and how we prepare for them.

Anxiety.

Anxiety feels a lot like stress but there is a crucial difference. Whereas stress is a reaction to what is happening now, anxiety relates to the future. This can be a real event that will likely take place, so some anxiety is a normal reaction. Let's say, you will go into hospital for an operation, you would expect a certain amount of apprehension. But if you lie awake at night worrying about imaginary health issues when you are perfectly healthy, that is unhelpful and will detract from your happiness in the here-and-now. Anxious people waste a lot of time and mental energy worrying about events that will probably never happen.

As fear drives anxiety, the anxious person will usually expect the worst-case outcome from a future event, whether that future event is likely to take place or is pure fantasy. The emotional mind does not differentiate between what will probably happen and what will not, so it will trigger a release of adrenaline in either event.

If the anxiety is because of a likely future event, such as the example I just mentioned of having an operation, the anxiety will go once the event has passed. But if the anxiety is fear of an improbable future event, then it is likely to become chronic because if the event never happens, you cannot get past it. Over time, the adrenaline in the body builds up and sometimes bursts out of its normal levels, causing a panic attack.

The term *panic attack* has entered popular language and is often used colloquially to describe feeling overwhelmed. But as anyone who has experienced one of these attacks will confirm, a real panic attack is truly terrifying. Typical symptoms include a racing heartbeat, feeling like you might die, shaking and sweating, feeling you are floating off from reality, and an immense sense of dread.

Although panic attacks have a trigger event, they are usually the result of long-term anxiety – they build up over time until they reach a critical level and explode. The methods you will learn in this book will reduce the chance of this happening to you, or lessen the chance of a recurrence if this has already taken place in your life.

Phobias are a form of irrational fear and a subsection of anxiety. I doubt it would be possible to list all the phobias, there are so many. Here are some common ones:

- Being in crowds
- Being alone
- Creatures, e.g. spiders and moths
- Social situations
- Open spaces
- Enclosed spaces
- Flying
- Germs and infections
- Public speaking
- Heights

Most people are prone to having a phobia or two. They are usually mild and are not especially troublesome. But sometimes they become central to people's lives. I have had numerous clients who suffer from agoraphobia or social anxiety and these issues can be serious impediments to having a fulfilling life.

Post-Traumatic Stress Disorder is a form of anxiety that comes from exposure to abuse or violence. Typical symptoms include flashbacks to past trauma, feeling constantly on alert to danger and feeling emotionally detached. I will not cover PTSD specifically, as it requires specialist support beyond the scope of this book. Having worked with PTSD clients, I believe the techniques in this book will help, but I would urge anyone who thinks they might have this disorder to seek medical help.

Negativity.

Everyone's life has its ups and downs. Negativity is a mindset where a person filters out the ups and only sees the downs. It will often have its roots in painful past events. The negative person will look for evidence that life is always like that and ignore any contrary evidence. A negative person will go to the supermarket with a long shopping list and become angry or frustrated about one thing being out of stock while ignoring the good news that all the other items on the list were in stock.

Negativity also comes from unrealistic expectations. People often lament that life isn't fair. Life clearly isn't fair in as much as some people are born with advantages that other people don't have. But that is how life is. What they really mean is that they don't have what they want in life. The expectation that life should provide what people expect causes much negativity. But the problem is not with life, it is with the gap between the person's expectations and reality. Instead of enjoying what they have, they become downbeat because of that gap, which is entirely of their own invention.

Where you find negativity, you will usually find its sidekick, procrastination. The negative person will reason that as life is just one long series of disappointments, why should you bother? Consequently, activity gives way to procrastination. Ironically, negative people often put a lot of thought and effort into doing very little.

This sets off an unfortunate cycle: procrastination leads to lack of achievement which leads to disappointment in life which leads right back to procrastination. And so it goes on. Many people spend their lives in this glum cycle of mediocrity.

Negativity takes the fun out of life, leaving the individual with feelings of emptiness, resentment and self-pity. But it's avoidable, and this book will show you how.

Finally in this chapter, I want to say a few words about depression. I left the word depression out of the title of this book because it would be wrong to suggest that you can turn around severe depression in 10 days. You cannot. It requires focused medical and therapeutic support.

However, the word depression covers a wide area. Not all depression is severe. Mild depression can come and go. It has many causes. These may be hormonal or because of a temporary imbalance in dopamine or serotonin, like *seasonally adjusted disorder*, which is a transitory form of depression triggered by low light levels in winter. Depression can be self-inflicted through the use of recreational drugs; it can be brought on by stress, anxiety and negativity; or conversely, those things can be symptoms of depression, so we need to be aware of that as we go through this book.

When many people say they are depressed, they mean they are temporarily in a low mood. This is often because of a disappointment such as losing a job or a relationship break-up. Low mood can feature feelings of hopelessness or despair, similar to depression, but unlike depression, low mood will lift in a matter of days or weeks. Nonetheless, it's an emotionally painful place to be while it's in your life. Using the tools in this book, you will cope much better when you find yourself in such a situation.

Stress, anxiety, negativity, and low mood are interrelated. If you are suffering from one of these, you will probably have them all at times, often at the same time. One of these conditions will trigger another, so it's common to get into what we often label with the cliché of a downward spiral. However, spirals don't have to go downwards. By treating one condition using the methods in this book, you can spark an improvement across the range and create an upward spiral of relief.

Deep Relaxation.

When you always have stress and anxiety in your life, relaxation is in short supply. You may believe that:

- You have no time to relax.
- Relaxation is a luxury
- You don't deserve to relax.
- If you relax, other people will judge you badly.
- Your agenda is too full to relax.
- Relaxed people are lazy.
- You have too many worries to relax.
- You will relax later, but first, you must hurry to do something.

However, I have news. All of the above are false. It's disinformation that your emotional mind pumps out.

Relaxation is a basic human right. Relaxation is almost as essential to your well-being as air and water. If you are denying yourself relaxation, only bad things will result. If you don't think you have time to relax, then consider that research shows these benefits of regular relaxation:

- Your body produces less adrenaline, so you will feel less stressed and anxious.
- Your blood sugar levels remain more balanced, so you will have fewer mood-extremes.
- You will sleep better and have more energy.
- Your blood pressure will be lower and you will be at reduced risk of heart disease.
- You are less likely to feel overwhelmed, angry or panicky.
- You will be able to concentrate and think more clearly.
- You will have better blood flow around your body resulting in fewer aches and pains.

That's an impressive list of benefits for doing something that's a pleasure. So it seems obvious, just relax. But if you are suffering from anxiety, you know it isn't that simple. You might have lost the ability to relax.

For instance, let's say it's the weekend and your kids want you to play a ball game with them. Sounds relaxing, right? But if you worry about work all the time, even while you are throwing the ball with your kids, your emotional mind will be telling you that you don't have time for this trivia. You think you need to get back to solving your problems, which makes you feel stressed in the present. You lose the simple pleasure of playing a game with your kids. This is a tragic way of feeling and all too common.

So in this chapter, I want to introduce you to the pleasure of Deep Relaxation, and I have a simple way for you to experience this. All you have to do is lie back and listen to the audio that goes with this book.

As these recordings are exclusive to readers of this book, you will be asked to set up an email log-in, which is easy and takes just a few seconds. This will get you access to all the downloads with this book and to the aftercare material and updates that I will be sending out by email over the next few months, which is explained more fully in on Day 10. In the unlikely event that you don't want to receive that, you can simply unsubscribe after you have downloaded the recording.

To get the downloads, go to:

www.subscribepage.com/emotions_audio

(Make sure you insert the underscore between emotions and audio, and enter youremail address correctly.)

When you have logged in, you will see a link to the mp3 audio downloads page. You will also get an email from me that gives you a link to the audios. Just in case you cannot get your audios with either of the above methods, send me an email to emotions.downloads@gmail.com and an autoresponder will email you back with an alternative link immediately. So you have three ways to get to your audios.

The first two mp3s are the deep relaxation downloads, called Waterfall Relaxation and Sunshine Relaxation. You will also see links to mindfulness and hypnotherapy recordings, but I suggest leaving those until you get to the appropriate chapters in this book. When you click on a link to an mp3, a play/pause widget will appear and your recording will play. If you want to download the recording to your device, click on the three dots on the right of the widget.

Now you have your recordings, you need to find 20 minutes when you can be in a comfortable place and you won't be disturbed. If you don't think you can find 20 minutes, then you are stressed, and it's even more important you make this time. If you have time for stress-inducing activities like watching the news or using social media, then you have time for relaxation.

Deep relaxation is not a chore or another task to check off your to-do list. It's a pleasure, it's living your life in the present moment. So find yourself somewhere quiet where you can sit or lie down in comfort and feel warm, as it's hard to relax when you're cold. Listen to the recordings on earbuds or headphones, close your eyes and enjoy. Antonia Ryan narrated the recordings, and her soft Irish voice is easy on the ear. You can listen to either or both recordings as often as you like. That's all you need to do.

It sounds easy and for most people, it is. I hope it will be easy and fun for you, too. But if you are used to being stressed, you might find this tricky at first. You might find you cannot focus on the words because your attention is habitually fragmented. You might find that you have the urge to get up and do something because your body is perpetually in fight-or-flight mode.

The more difficult you find it to relax with these recordings, the more tension you have in your body, so the more reason to persevere with listening to the recordings, and the others which follow in this book.

That's the end of Day One. You should have much to think about and do because of what you have read so far and I hope you can see why I recommend reading this book over

10 days. So give yourself time to digest today's chapters and give your emotional brain time to absorb a new way of reacting to your world.

Tomorrow we will get into some fabulous strategies to help you find emotional balance and happiness.

Day Two.

Thoughts.

Have you ever tried observing your thoughts?

I have. It's a curious experience. I first came across this idea when I was working in public health. The management sent me on a course to learn how meditation can be used in counselling. When I arrived, the trainer told me to look at my thoughts.

At first, I couldn't understand what I was supposed to be doing. How could I look at my own thoughts? Surely, you are thinking all the time, how can you stop and look at that? Surely, you are your thoughts?

Well, as it turned out, I could look at my thoughts. It took some time to get the hang of. It's a knack. Essentially, you sit calmly and watch the thoughts as they appear in your head. You don't try to force anything, you let your thoughts come and go as they please.

What I saw surprised me.

I guess I had always assumed that thinking was a continuous process where your thoughts moved in a smooth sequence. But as I discovered, it's not like that at all. It's all rather higgledy-piggledy. First, it wasn't continuous, there were gaps when I wasn't consciously thinking anything. Second, the thoughts were disconnected, flitting from one subject to another. It was all rather messy. My logical mind wanted to get involved and tidy up, but the trick to doing this is in keeping your logical mind offline, so to speak, so you can observe what's going on.

The big lesson I drew from all this was that I am not my thoughts. I can exist, at least for a short time, without consciously thinking. Thoughts are events that take place in your mind. Some are useful but some make no sense at all. And they are not facts or instructions. You don't have to do what they say. You can be selective.

But most of us are unselective. Not because we are foolish, but because we didn't know you could choose. Nobody told us. Our parents never told us because they never knew, either.

Your emotional mind is firing out random thoughts all the time. Some are useful and some are just plain wrong. Imagine you are trying to cross a busy street. Your emotional mind will be concerned. It rightly senses danger and fires out warnings to you. You feel apprehensive, a little fearful. In this situation, those feelings are helpful. On that busy street, fear makes you pay attention to the potential danger of being erased out of existence by a passing truck.

But if you fear leaving your house to go to your local shop because your emotional brain tells you that fictitious dangers await you, that's unhelpful, that's where anxiety comes from.

If you go through your day accepting these thoughts as facts or instructions, you will experience stress. When most people think about stress, they assume it's from external pressures. That's true, but only part of the story. We all have stressful situations every day. But not all stress is generated by other people. You generate stress from inside, too, if you act on your thoughts without being selective.

In the therapeutic groups I run, we have a name for the misleading messages sent out from your emotional brain that generate stress: thought-bombs. They are the untruths that, if you accept them as fact, will explode sending your emotions scattering. Here are some examples of typical thought-bombs:

- I never do anything right.
- You can see by his face that he hates me.
- Everyone is so unfair to me.
- That shouldn't be allowed.
- I was born unlucky.
- Everyone thinks I'm stupid.
- I can't be happy until I fit in that dress.
- I need a better car so people will respect me.
- I can't relax until I get this finished.
- If I don't pass this exam, my career will be over.
- No one will ever love me.
- She hasn't called. She must want to dump me.
- If it rains, it'll ruin my whole holiday.

Your emotional mind will fire out thought-bombs when it feels insecure. It has a habit of looking at the worst-case. It's not deliberately trying to mislead you, but it's very reactive, it doesn't stop to think – that's your job.

So, how do you deal with a thought-bomb? The first thing is to recognize that the incoming thought is potentially a thought-bomb. You can spot them because they are always accompanied by a sudden change or deterioration in your mood. When a thought like this pops up in your mind, take a pause before you react. It might help to visualize yourself mentally stepping back from the thought and inspecting it. Consider, is this thought true? Is there any evidence? If the answer is no, it's a thought-bomb, so label it. Say clearly to yourself, this is a thought-bomb. And that's how you defuse them. When you label them, you expose what they are, you take away their destructive power.

I would like you to practise this today. Being able to step back from a thought, evaluate it, and label it is a core skill in balancing your emotional life.

It will take time to get used to using this skill. In the past, you have always reacted as soon as a thought hits you. It's your default. So at first, many thought-bombs will get past your defence, explode, and cause you emotional pain. You may realize later what has happened. If this occurs, don't criticize yourself for letting a destructive thought get the better of you. Replacing your old, unhelpful default with a new and better one will take time. So when you realize you have been thought-bombed, look at what happened and see if you can learn something from the experience.

How often do you get thought-bombed? It might surprise you how often one of these plausible lies comes your way. Label it and move on.

The Rule of Three.

Anxiety can come from events. If you have an important interview to attend, or a presentation to do, or an exam to take, then some anxiety might even be helpful in that it would spur you on to do your best. But for more chronic forms of anxiety, where you are losing sleep worrying about things that might never even happen, then the source of the anxiety is within.

So how did it get there in the first place?

The most likely cause is criticism. You were criticized as a child. You were criticized as you grew up. You are criticized now. Unfair criticism is hard to take, it leads to anger, even outrage, both toxic emotions. But even valid criticism hurts.

Imagine you are going to see your boss for your regular employee assessment. You want to hear praise, since you want that pleasurable burst of dopamine - your body's own natural feel-good chemical - that you get when someone says something nice about you. So when your boss praises you, your emotional brain opens up the dopamine valve and you feel great. You hang on to every approving word.

But when your boss starts talking about action points for your development, your heart sinks. Your emotional mind sends out an urgent warning that you are going to hear something you won't like. The dopamine supply gets switched off. The logical side of your brain gets into action, telling you that this is good for you, constructive criticism will help you become better at your job, so you should keep smiling, be positive and learn. But it's raining inside your emotional mind and your feelings are getting soaked in disappointment.

If we are honest with ourselves, we all struggle with criticism. No matter how well-intentioned, it always stings a little bit. Even I'm not exempt. If someone criticizes my work, I treat it constructively; I look at the criticism analytically and consider what I can learn from it, but it still leaves a small bruise on my ego. So when we are sharply or unfairly criticised, that really hurts.

Your emotional mind wants to shield you from that suffering, so it will tell you that the person who is the source of your discomfort is unjust. It can make you resentful, another toxic emotion. It drives you into negativity if you think that whatever you do is never good enough to please some people.

Criticism also leads to perfectionism because, on a subconscious level, you reason that if you are perfect, you will be above criticism, which will take the pain away. So you measure yourself against unrealistically high standards.

It is an irony that people can be perfectionistic and negative at the same time. Such people would not think of themselves as perfectionists at all - they usually regard themselves as being flawed and often have a poor self-image. However, they are driven to behaving in a perfectionistic way to avoid more hurtful criticism. They believe that they can only do that by never making a mistake.

If the source of these unrealistic standards is another person, say an employer or intimate partner, then you need to look at that relationship and whether it's turned toxic on you. But frequently the source is what we believe are other people's standards for us, so you are second-guessing what someone else thinks. If you try to live up those standards, which could be entirely in your imagination, then you will get beaten up by your own beliefs.

You will always be on a loser trying to be perfect because perfection in human behaviour is a matter of opinion, not fact, and opinions change. Also, we all have different opinions. Perfection is a constantly shifting target. Trying to be perfect is like nailing down water.

Yet people set themselves delusory targets in the belief it will put them beyond the pain of criticism. This opens up the door to anxiety as you worry about achieving those targets, and stress will eat at you when you try to measure up to them, as the adrenaline is pumping.

Perfectionism makes us negative. As you will never be perfect, you have set yourself up for continual disappointment, so negativity can become your default state, as you believe you will never be good enough. The fact usually is that you were good enough all along, the problem was that you set the bar at a height impossible for you ever to jump over, no matter how hard you tried.

It's easy to confuse perfection with success. You might feel you have to be perfect to succeed in life, then are down on yourself for not being perfect when you don't succeed. But success is not perfection. As successful people know, success is messy.

Take, for example, top sportspeople. They will train relentlessly to make their technique as good as possible, but they know that it's how they handle failure that makes them great. A top footballer will accept there are days when he is off form or when the opposition are just too good. But that doesn't mean he cannot win trophies over the course of a season. A great golfer might spend hours every day trying to get her swing as near as possible to perfect, but will know that some days she will hit the ball into the trees, and success comes from how she bounces back from those situations when her swing is off.

So today, I want you to look at your life and identify if the pursuit of perfection is causing yourself pain. Are you trying to live up to the expectations of someone else? Are you trying to achieve standards that are fanciful for you? The sad thing is that if you are trying to attain perfection in any area, that if you do momentarily succeed, it will not feel so great. Why? Because you want to keep it and for it to become the default in your life, but it will always be a fleeting thing.

If you find that you are trying to achieve the impossible, perhaps through being the perfect parent, employee, partner or whatever, try this. Instead of being a perfectionist, try being an imperfectionist. This is how:

Because you are human, you will make mistakes. This is non-negotiable, it will happen. But rather than regarding this as a failure or evidence that there is something wrong with you, see it as proof of your humanity. It validates your membership of the human race. No human is perfect.

Making mistakes helps you improve. Ask any successful person and they will tell you the same: they learned more from their mistakes than anything else – they built their success on their mistakes. Look at the most successful team in your favourite sport. Have they always been the most successful? Probably not. There will have been times in their past when they played badly and had an awful season. But to have become successful, they will have learned from their mistakes.

You improve from making mistakes as well. Think about any skill you have learned in your life: riding a bike, kicking a ball, baking a cake, flying a kite, driving a car, whatever you have learned, you learned from the mistakes you made.

So, today I want you to take it as a given that you will make three mistakes. It will happen because you are human. When you make a mistake today, just think to yourself "Great, that's one checked off my three." So keep counting until you reach your three, then congratulate yourself on your humanity instead of beating yourself up.

Then look for the value in what you have done. How can your mistakes help you? Let's say, you made a howling error at work and your boss reprimanded you, usually this might result in you criticizing yourself and getting resentful at your boss. This is counterproductive. So if something like this happens to you, in future I want you firstly to let yourself off the hook. Instead, congratulate yourself as you have just chalked up one of your three mistakes for the day. Secondly, don't waste your time with having a resentment against anyone who criticises you. Resentment is a toxic emotion that will give you even more pain. (In fact, it's so toxic, I have devoted a chapter to resentment later in this book.)

Next, look at that error in a non-judgemental way. What can you learn from what happened that you can turn to your benefit in future? How can this disappointment lead to success at a later date? What could you do differently next time that situation arises? If the mistake has revealed a weakness in you, how can you turn that weakness into a strength?

Then look at three things that you have done well in your day. If you have had a horrible day, you might dismiss this idea, thinking you have done nothing well. But that kind of thinking is the path to negativity, and it's also misleading because if you look closely, you will find three things you did well in even the worst kind of day.

This is because of *The Rule Of Three*, which states that in any day, you will make at least three errors and do at least three things well.

I leave it up to you to decide what constitutes something you have done well and what is a mistake, as this is relative to where you are in your life at the moment. But it's important that what you think is a success or an error is genuinely your idea, not what you think you should do to please someone else. Use your own standards, not other people's.

When you have identified the three things you did well, look at them in the same non-judgmental way you looked at your errors and ask yourself what you can learn from what went right. Can you do more of the thing that went well?

So, for instance, if you made a meal for the family that everyone enjoyed, look at what ingredients and cooking methods you used and ask yourself what you did that was successful that you can do again. If you have a pleasant time with a loved one, ask yourself what pleased you both and what you could repeat that you could enjoy again. If you had a good morning at work and things seemed to flow, ask yourself why that was and what happened that could work again.

It's helpful to get into the habit of analysing successes and errors dispassionately. Try looking at what happened as mere events in your life, whether good or bad isn't important. Look at what happened with a sense of curiosity rather than being judgmental. This keeps your emotional mind quiet, allowing your logical mind to do its job. Your emotional mind will also turn down the supply of adrenaline, helping you feel calmer, and turn up the supply of serotonin, giving you more feelings of contentment.

Finally in this chapter, I would mention one question that always crops up in training groups I run when we discuss *The Rule of Three*. Someone will always ask, "What if I make over three mistakes?" The answer is that you can congratulate yourself even more because you have just given yourself more opportunities to learn and improve.

Dynamic De-stress.

With arguments going on between your logical and emotional minds and thought-bombs exploding, your head can be a wild place. So in this chapter, we will go through a tried and tested technique for turning down all that stressful activity in your head, anytime and anywhere you need it. This simple system works:

- When you are alone.
- When you are in a crowd.
- When you are working.
- When you cannot sleep.
- When you are angry.
- When you feel overwhelmed.
- When you are fearful.
- When your head is running out of control.
- When you want a few moments of emotional respite.

I have taught this technique in training workshops many times. Usually, there will be a group of people who have all turned up with a miscellany of emotional troubles. They will often have been referred by their doctor or other care agencies. They will all have anxiety and stress from busy, often chaotic lives. Some will have emotional pain from past trauma. Many will be in challenging relationships. Some will have substance misuse issues. But they all have one thing in common: they want some peace in their heads.

We call the technique I am about to describe the *Dynamic De-stress*. It's really quite simple. You can learn it easily today. I think its simplicity is its strength. I have tried more complex methods with clients and they have worked well in the peaceful environment of one of my workshops. But they have proved too convoluted when life gets frantic in the outside world.

When you are under pressure, your mind is spinning, and emotions are flying every which way, you need something dependable you can hang on to. The *Dynamic De-stress* is that. This is how it works.

To begin, find a comfortable place to sit where you will be undisturbed for a few minutes. You will be able to use the Dynamic De-stress in a variety of situations, but on this first occasion, it's easier to have the chance to concentrate without distractions.

This practice has three parts. Firstly, I want you to feel grounded. You can do this sitting, standing or lying down.

If you are sitting, get comfortable, preferably with your feet flat on the floor and your hands palms-down on the arms of the chair, or flat on your legs. Feel that your weight is evenly distributed. Sit back in the chair. Do not sit on the edge, as this is a fight-or-flight posture, which is not what we want. Allow your weight to sink into the chair so you feel balanced and grounded.

If you are lying down, lie flat on your back with your spine straight so that your weight is evenly distributed on either side. Have your legs slightly apart and your arms at your side. Allow your weight to sink into the surface below you.

If you are standing, have your feet shoulder-width apart, giving you a solid posture, with your spine vertical but not stiff. You might find that having your hands purposefully on your hips adds to the feeling of a solid posture. Feel your weight sinking into the ground through your feet. You might find on this first occasion it helps to close your eyes or to look at a neutral point and allow your gaze to soften.

Next, I want you to tense up all the muscles in your body as much as you can. That's right, tense up all the muscles in your body, from your head to your feet, at the same time. Hold your breath, your hands will be in tight fists, you might especially feel the tension it in your neck and shoulders. You should feel your body shaking slightly. Keep your whole body as tense as you can, without breathing out, for at least five seconds, ten seconds if you can. Then release all your muscles at the same time and let your breath out. This should feel a wave of relief and your whole body should feel loose and relaxed for a few moments. Try repeating this once or twice. When you relax your muscles, you should find the looseness pleasant.

If you experience difficulty in tensing up your whole body, focus just on tensing up your neck and shoulders for a few seconds and then letting go. Your neck and shoulders in particular store stress.

Next, place the palm of one hand on your stomach. Observe what happens when you breathe. Does your hand move out or stay unmoved? If it remains unmoved, you are breathing into your upper chest, which indicates stress. If this is the case, imagine you are breathing right down into your stomach. You should feel your stomach inflate and your hand move forward. Of course, you cannot really breathe into your stomach, but imagining that you are means that you are using your full lung capacity and your diaphragm moves out. This will slow down your breathing, making it more rhythmical and less stressed, and you will get the maximum oxygen into your system.

Focus on breathing deep into your diaphragm, then breathing out, and repeat. This sounds easy but, particularly at emotionally stressful times, your thoughts will quickly intrude and draw your attention away from your breathing, resulting in you becoming tenser again. To help with this, count one on the in-breath, two on the out-breath, three on the in-breath, four on the out-breath and so on. You can make a game of this – try to see how high you can count before your thoughts distract you. When you realize you have been distracted, simply go back to one and start again. Repeat as long as you like.

So to summarize, the Dynamic De-stress has three parts:

- Stand, sit or lie with your weight evenly distributed. Feel your weight sinking into and supported by the surface below you.
- Tense your body and hold your breath for at least 5 seconds, then release and repeat.
- Breathe deep into your diaphragm, counting your breaths in and out. Continue for as long as desired.

The Dynamic De-stress defuses thought-bombs and dilutes toxic emotions. It can stop you from doing something you might regret later. It calms you, so you can think straight. Repeated use lessens the risk of panic attacks.

I would like you to try this a few times today. You find that once you get the hang of it, you can use it in many situations. You need not be alone. You can tense your muscles subtly so other people don't notice. You can breathe deeply into your diaphragm without attracting attention. This makes the technique versatile. You can use it while you are waiting for an appointment, standing in the supermarket check-out, walking down the road, sitting in a meeting at work, and while other people or events seem to be conspiring to stress you out. It's your secret weapon to keep your emotions balanced when life is frantic.

You have much to practice today: identifying and labelling thought-bombs, tracking three errors and three things you did well, and using the Dynamic De-stress. So don't continue reading, start doing. You might need a notepad to keep track of your progress. Remember, this is not work, this is living your life. Have fun with it.

Then tomorrow, we get deeper into the cool stuff

Day Three.

The Scale of Ten.

If you have ever visited a therapist or counselling service regarding stress or emotional issues, it's likely they asked you to rate things on a numerical scale. Most commonly, a therapist will ask you to give an answer out of ten. The question might be something like, "On a scale of one to ten, where ten means wonderful and one means terrible, how would you rate your state of mind today?"

This is a system called scaling, and it's so useful because:

- It gives the therapist an immediate snapshot of how the client is.
- It gives the client motivation to reflect on themselves.
- It provides a way of recording and monitoring progress over weeks or months.

When I was working in therapeutic services, I carried out clinical assessments with new clients. These assessments varied in complexity and content according to the specific issues of the client. But there were three things I was mandated to ask everyone:

- A score for their opinion of their mental health.
- A score for their opinion of their physical health.
- A score for their opinion of their overall quality of life.

The score for their mental health was about how they felt that day - what their emotional state was at that moment in time. For many people, they don't think they have mental health, they only talk about mental health in terms of being ill, like it's a bad thing. But just as we all have physical health, we all have mental health and it needs looking after.

Getting a score for the client's physical health was also important in understanding what was going on in their head. If the score was low, I would ask why, because what goes on with your body impacts on your mind. If you have physical pain, that's likely to bring down your emotional state, so finding out if it's transitory or chronic gives an indicator of how long it's likely to affect your feelings and what action can be taken.

The score for overall quality of life took into account such things as getting on with family and friends and the ability to enjoy yourself. It's curious how some people who seem to have everything going for them can feel they have a low quality of life, while people with multiple issues and disadvantages can feel life is cool. It just goes to show that how you view your life is more important than who you are or what you have.

If you record these scores over time, you will have a way to monitor your progress, so I would suggest asking yourself these questions now and making a note of them. At the end of the ten days, you can see if things have improved. Then I would suggest you answer them again every few weeks to check how you are. If a score has changed, whether up or down, ask yourself what has changed. If you are doing something new that's making an improvement, could you do more of it? Conversely, if something has brought you down, can you change what's happening?

I would also suggest you use scaling to monitor your feelings over the ten days of this book. At the very least, record a rating for yourself once a day for how good you feel in your head. Even better, do it several times a day at regular intervals. Record what you are doing at that time. You might find this revealing.

For instance, if your lowest score of the day is always when you first get up in the morning, ask yourself why that is and if you can do something about it. Do you need to change your bedtime routine? Are you using a recreational drug in the evening to improve your mood, which is leading to a low mood the following day?

There's another great use for scaling. During your day, there will be many times when thoughts and emotions are calling for your attention. Scale it. Ask yourself, how beneficial is this for me today? Give it a score. I use the word "beneficial" because what you might want to do at any given time may be different from what would be in your interests. So, if you feel like staying in bed and watching videos on your iPhone all day instead of going to work, scale it. In terms of desirable, staying in bed might score well. But in terms of beneficial, going to work and being paid probably hits a higher score.

When a thought pops into your head from the emotional part of your brain, it's all too easy to treat it like a command. But it's nothing of the kind. It's just a thought. And as it's come from your emotional brain, it's quite likely to be random and not helpful. It could be a thought-bomb. Having the ability to see that is a crucial skill to develop which will benefit you forever.

Yesterday, we discussed imagining yourself standing back from your thoughts and inspecting them, then asking yourself if they were really true. Did you try that exercise? Did it work? Or did you get wrapped up in the hurly-burly of your day and forget to do it? Whatever happened, let's try again today, and use your new skill of scaling to help. All you have to do is look at your thoughts and give them a score out of ten for how beneficial they are to you at that point in time. This is why it works:

Firstly, when you stop to scale a thought, you put a vital pause between the arrival of that thought and taking action. That pause will bring down your stress levels right away. Why? Because a major cause of stress is acting immediately on your thoughts if you don't have a moment to reflect. Stressed people are reacting all the time. Random ideas fly out of their emotional brains endlessly, pushing them around and dominating their time. If you are reacting, rather than reflecting, you will soon get exhausted, which is how stressed people feel, and that's why. You cannot keep up the pace to react to your emotional brain's huge daily output of erratic ideas. But if you have a pause to scale an incoming idea, you have the chance to spot whether the thought is really a thought-bomb that's about to blow up your day.

Secondly, when you give it a score, you can see right away whether it's worth your attention. Remember, you are scoring how beneficial it is for you at that time. Let's take a simple example. Imagine you are an office worker, you've been at work half an hour, and you have a ton of reports to input on the office database before lunch. Suddenly, the thought hits you, "Hey, I need a sandwich." At some points in the day, you could scale that quite high, after all, you need to eat. But hold on a minute, it hasn't been that long since breakfast, you're not that hungry. You can only scale that at maybe a two, whereas getting on with the inputting is an eight or nine. In reality, the sandwich thought wasn't because of genuine hunger, it was your emotional brain saying, "The hell with the inputting, I want an excuse to procrastinate." If you had reacted, bought a sandwich you didn't even want and wasted half an hour, you would have fallen behind with your work and got stressed trying to finish work on time. But the act of scaling stopped all that.

The random nature of your emotional mind's output can easily distract you. For instance, I can see in the mirror right now that I need a haircut. I'm in charge of what I do today, so I could turn off my laptop, go for a walk into the town and get it cut. No one will object. It seems like quite a reasonable thing to do. But if I scale it, I would only put it about a three. It's not that desperate, it could easily wait a few days.

Whereas sticking to my writing schedule so I get my book finished on time is a ten for me.

So there is no debate in my head. Using scaling helps me cut through the endless chitter-chatter coming from the back of my brain. I will finish my writing target for the morning before I do anything else. Then I will do the thing that scores next highest. Checking the email from readers of my books scores higher than a haircut, so that's next. But if I had allowed my emotional brain to distract me, I could be sitting in the barber's right now, wondering how I managed to blow my writing schedule for the day.

Applying the Scale of Ten, therefore, takes a lot of self-inflicted stress out of your life and makes your day easier because it also prioritizes the order you need to do things. It makes getting the most beneficial stuff done easy. If you don't do everything that's on your to-do list for the day, it's no drama, because you've done what really matters. Getting my hair cut wasn't especially beneficial for me today. But if I had failed to do my word count for the day, I would feel unnecessary stress.

These are small examples of how acting reactively can upset the balance of your day. Stress and anxiety come into play without need because of one small decision. Now imagine if you are reacting impulsively to the random thoughts coming from your emotional brain all day long. Image how stressful the cumulative effect of many such decisions would be? In fact, you might not need to imagine because, if you are a typical member of humanity, this is probably what you do every day. Most of us are like this by default and will go through life without realizing why we keep sabotaging ourselves unless we learn a better way.

Also, people make spontaneous decisions based on random emotional thoughts that can have a major impact on their lives. Customers can make immense financial commitments, like buying a car or even a house, because of an emotional thought while they're in the showroom or show home. Salespeople know this and sales training is largely about how to press the right psychological buttons so that customers think with their emotional brains rather than the logical one.

Has that ever happened to you? Or maybe you have been trapped in a difficult relationship for years because you acted on an emotional thought once and asked the wrong person out. Perhaps you lost a job because you reacted rather than reflected while working on an important project. Maybe you even got arrested for something that your emotional brain told you was a reasonable thing to do.

When these things happen to my clients, they usually say the classic words, "It seemed like a good idea at the time." But it wasn't.

So today I would like you to scale your thoughts and develop this skill that will change your life. You should find that your decision making improves dramatically and will soon become a natural part of your thinking. Then, just as quickly, your levels of stress decline as you eliminate potentially self-sabotaging behaviours with ease. You might wonder how you ever managed without using scaling.

What If?

"I wish I could shut my head up," said Emma, "but I just can't stop worrying about money since Joe left. He's being difficult about paying maintenance. The kids and I are relying on my income at the moment."

"So, is money tight?" I asked.

"Well, not right now. In fact, I always earned more than him. Since he's gone, money's been okay."

"So, why worry about money?"

"Well, what if I lost my job? Everything relies on me now. If I lost my job, what would we do? It would be like a house of cards falling down. I can't sleep worrying about it. It's affecting my health. The kids are picking up on it, and they're getting anxious."

"Is your job in danger?"

"Well, not right now. But what if that changed? What if the company was bought out and the new owners put in their own people and decided they didn't need me? Then what would we do?"

"Tell me something," I asked. "On a scale of one to ten - where ten is highly probable and one is very unlikely - how likely is it that would happen, let's say, in the next twelve months?"

"In the next twelve months? Well, I guess it would be a one."

"And, knowing that, how well do you think you will sleep tonight?"

"Better!"

Emma ran the administration for a well-known property company. She had been there for ten years and knew how the company worked like no one else. She was the glue that held the business together. If another company took over, the new owners would be desperate to keep her on. If they released her, the owners would have to compensate her considerably. Yet a highly unlikely, worst-case possibility was keeping her awake. Her husband leaving had shaken her confidence and a "What if?" had thought-bombed her. Her mind had gone into an unnecessary crisis-planning mode.

What-ifs are most likely to hit you when something unexpected has happened or when something is not as it usually is.

Your mind does an amazing job with problem-solving. We humans thrive on this. We do puzzles and play games to challenge our problem-solving abilities - we do it for fun. But a difficulty occurs when a what-if hits you about a future event that might never happen. Your mind goes off to solve the problem. But it cannot. There isn't a solution to this kind of what-if. Your mind cannot solve a theoretical future event because there is an infinite number of variables that could come into play. All the mind can do is come up with changing scenarios.

Nevertheless, your mind carries on trying to solve it for you. Then you feel that your head is going in circles. You cannot stop ruminating about outcomes. You cannot sleep. Your stomach churns. You feel on edge. In short, you have anxiety.

What-if speculation about theoretical future events is a prime cause of stress. Clients never tell me they have been kept awake at night because their mind has been ruminating on what-if scenarios with happy outcomes, it's always fear of disaster.

What-ifs always seem to ask, "What if something goes wrong?" We could equally ask, "What if something goes right?" But generally, we don't because our survival instinct tells us to expect the worst. It's trying to protect us. It knows that if we live in fear, we are more likely to survive. But in our modern world, this can ruin people's lives rather than save them.

Take Arthur. Anxiety plagues his thinking and the what-ifs love to mess around with his emotions. If his wife is 15 minutes late arriving home, he will start to worry. What if something is wrong? After half an hour, his mind will be speculating that her car has broken down. He wants to call her, but fears that if he calls while she is driving, he could cause an accident. After 45 minutes, he is pacing the floor, his heart is racing, and his mind is spinning. The what-if thoughts are poking a sharp stick into the open wound of his deepest fears. He is convinced that something awful has happened. What if a crash has occurred and she is in a pool of blood, dying in a wreck? Then he hears her car on the gravel and falls to his knees in relief. She walks in with the groceries she had bought on the way home, wondering why Arthur looks so emotional.

Arthur is no fool. The logical part of his mind had told him that in all probability, she was fine. He knew he was being irrational. But this logical thought had been lost in the hubbub from the what-ifs. The stress he felt and the reactions of his body were very real, yet the cause had been a fantasy. Yes, there could have been an accident and his worst fears could have come true, but just as in Emma's case, the chance of it being true well was below one out of ten.

The what-ifs are not restricted to the future. They can play havoc with your peace of mind by using memories of the past, too. But whereas what-ifs about the future provoke fear of events they may never happen, with the past they cause regret, sadness or anger about events that have already taken place.

What happens is that your mind ruminates about a past event that troubles you, maybe just a minor matter, or a serious trauma, or something in between. You ask yourself, "What if that hadn't happened?" "What if I had done something differently?" "What if she hadn't done that?" And so on. It could also occur in the form of an if-only, as in "If only things had been different."

When one of these thought-bombs hits you, it again causes your brain to go into problem-solving mode. Your mind will try to solve the issue. But it cannot, since no amount of thought can change an event that has already happened. But it will keep trying, ending in pointless hours of churning over events you cannot change, and another sleepless night.

If a truly awful event has happened recently in your life, this rumination will be inevitable and part of the grieving process, you will need time to heal, and you might need counselling. Some life-events are so terrible that we never completely get over them. But we can still move forward into a happier state of mind.

Most of the time, dwelling on distressing past events is self-defeating. It will not put them right: it will keep you in that painful place. You can use your mind more constructively and dwell on happier things. I'm sure at this point some readers will be thinking something like, "It's all very well for the writer of this book to say that. Doing it is a different matter." And you would be right. It's a challenge, and later in this book, we will be looking at powerful techniques to deal with such situations.

But let's take this one day at a time. Today I would like you to turn your attention to two things.

Firstly, I want you to be on the alert for what-if and if-only thought-bombs. When one hits you, label it right away. The more you practice doing this, the easier it will become to dismiss them. Labelling them helps you see that they are simply thoughts and you have a choice whether you engage with them are not. Just because a thought comes into your head doesn't mean you have to take any notice of it.

Secondly, use the Scale of Ten, as I did with Emma, for hypothetical future events that are causing you distress. It might also help if you add a timescale. How likely is this to happen today, or this week, or this year, or even in your lifetime? If the score is low, ask yourself if this really is worth taking up your valuable time, causing you distress or keeping you awake? Probably not.

However, if something scores highly, that's where your attention should be, but even then, there is no need to ruminate endlessly. You can file it away until an appropriate time comes to deal with it. You don't need to worry about how you will deal with important matters that are causing you stress because we will be covering that in this book also. For today, I just want you to practise dismissing the low scoring thoughts as irrelevant and a waste of time, and filing away the important, high-scoring thoughts until I show you how to deal with them.

You can also apply the scaling system to past events. For example, if a disturbing event happened in your childhood, how likely is it that agonizing about it now will put it right? Scale it out of ten - it has to be a zero. Or if you have had a relationship split and the other person has left the state and married someone else, how probable is it that turning it over and over in your mind will change things? I think that's another zero.

If you can put some thought into these simple strategies, you will be making good progress in mastering such stressful thinking in the ten days of this book.

Day Four.

Active Awareness.

Worrying obsessively about the future and churning over past pain is a common characteristic of people with stress and anxiety. It robs you of contentment and drains the joy out of your life. Your sleep suffers. It makes you feel ill. You might need medication. This happens when your mind is always focused on the future or the past.

If this describes you, then you may feel that it is your normal state. You don't like it, but it's your default. However, it hasn't always been that way.

When you were very young, you were full of curiosity for the world you found yourself in. If you watch young children playing with toys, they are totally absorbed in the present, in a carefree state. And so were you once.

But then something happened during childhood or perhaps later in adolescence. Maybe you were frequently criticized and you learned to be anxious. As you have already learned in this book, criticism is a major cause of anxiety. You learn to question whether you are good enough to carry out your normal tasks. You worry about the future because you have discovered the future could contain more criticism, leading to emotional torment and self-doubt.

Maybe someone in your life treated you harshly and you discovered stress. Your mind turned over injustices that had happened to you and you worried about what might happen next. You learned to experience toxic emotions like regret, shame and resentment. Over time, you lost that curiosity for the world and your playfulness.

People without these issues spend most of their time living in the present. They have managed to reach adulthood having retained that curiosity and playfulness. The present is intrinsically interesting, so focusing on the here and now is no effort. When they think of the future, it's to plan, not to worry. If they think about past mistakes, it's to learn, not to beat themselves up. They still experience anxiety, stress, and emotional pain, as everyone does to some extent, but it doesn't consume them.

You too can live in that way and enjoy a much more satisfying life. The trick is to get back that playfulness and curiosity about your world. If you re-learn how to be fully engaged in the present most of the time, you will achieve this.

You have probably heard advice to live in the present. It sounds good, even blissful. You might have tried it. But as you are reading this book, it's likely you have had limited success with living in the present moment. This is a concept that makes sense to your logical mind, but if your emotional mind is throwing out many thought-bombs about how you don't have time for the present, it will undermine you. Instead, the adrenaline will be pumping and your head will spin with thoughts of a project at work, or what to make the kids for dinner, or how you will pay the mortgage, or whether you will be able to go on vacation this year, and so on ad infinitum – all stuff that will pull you away from the present and the peace of mind that goes with it.

But I have a solution.

In this chapter, we will look at a marvellous way to consciously re-connect with your present. It's a practice that, if used regularly, will quickly help you de-stress and enjoy the experience of the here and now. What's more, it's easy and fun.

I call it *Active Awareness*.

Before we get into how the practice works, though, I want to try a brief exercise with you. Think of a building that you know well, somewhere you visit frequently. It could be a friend's house, a place of work, a shop you use often, or a favourite café, for instance.

Have you chosen somewhere? Good. Now I want you to think about the walls in that place. Are they flat, textured or painted? What colour are they? If they are patterned, what exactly is the pattern? Are there any pictures, and if so, what do the pictures depict? Now think about the ceilings and answer the same questions. And how about the floors, what are they like? You should know, you have walked on them often enough.

Unless there are some striking features about the place that stand out in your mind, you might find it difficult to answer these questions with any certainty, even though you have seen these walls, ceilings and floors many times. You might even struggle to answer these questions about the rooms in your own home with 100% certainty, unless you are the person who did the decorating.

My point is that there is a huge amount in our world that we do not take in, and the more you are in your own head, rather than engaging with your present experience, the more you will miss. You can always spot the people on the street who are churning things over in their heads, they are the people who are looking at their feet while they are walking. They are oblivious to 95% of their world, as they are disconnected with the present. (Next time you find yourself looking at your feet while you are walking along the street, you will remember this book!)

Active awareness connects you to your world. This is how it works:

Set aside some time to do this on the first occasion you try this practice. I don't want you to feel in a rush. Stressed people feel they need to rush everything. If you can get out of the habit of behaving in a stressed way, you'll feel less stressed.

I want you to go to a place where you can observe your world. It doesn't have to be anywhere unusual. You could just go for a walk around the block, or sit in a park or a busy restaurant.

Next, I want you to really tune in to what your senses are telling you. What can you hear? I mean really hear. Not just the obvious. What's the closest sound and the most distant? What's the loudest and quietest? If you are walking, can you hear your clothes rustling and the sound of your steps, and the subtle sound changes as you move from one surface to another? If you are sitting down in a public place, what sounds do you hear from people walking past?

Now turn your attention to your vision. What can you see? I mean in detail. Look closely at the textures of buildings, fabrics, people's skin and the detailed shapes of plants. Soak in the colours. Observe exactly how people move. If you see something funny, don't forget to smile, it's the best way to relax your facial muscles. If you're walking down a familiar street, remember to look up. You might be surprised by all the detail you missed when you were looking at your feet.

How about your sense of touch? Can you feel your clothes sliding over your body as you move? Can you feel the constantly changing sensations in your feet as you walk? Can you detect air movement and small fluctuations in temperature on your skin? Really open yourself up to your senses. Let the sensations of the present moment wash over you. Try to find that sense of curiosity you had about the world when you were a child.

As you do this, you will have thoughts of the future or the past pop into your head. When you realize this has happened and your mind has begun brooding about something again, just say "Not now" and refocus on your senses. Do that every time your thoughts distract you from the present experience. If your emotional mind wants you to worry about something, well, you can worry later, if you must.

It's been a few years since I first tried this, which was when I was walking into work from my car one morning. This was a walk I knew well, or at least I thought I did. The number of sounds I had never noticed before and all the detail of the streets and buildings I had previously missed amazed me. I remember it clearly even now.

Once you get the hang of Active Awareness, you can use it anytime. When you are doing a routine task, really open up to what you are doing. You can use it at work. If you are in a meeting, instead of worrying about what everyone thinks about you, which is probably what you normally do, try to focus on exactly how people speak as well as what they say, how they move, little gestures. You're not being judgemental, you are being observant and fully involved in the moment. If you are driving, you will be a safer driver if you are fully present in what you are doing. Have you ever driven somewhere and suddenly realized your mind is elsewhere, you can't remember the journey, you have been driving on autopilot? That's how an anxious person drives. But you don't have to be an anxious person now. I want you to practise Active Awareness as much as you can, experiment with it, enjoy it.

Consider using Active Awareness when you usually reach for something to engage you, such as watching TV or turning on social media. Those activities are likely to increase your stress. I mean, when was the last time you finished watching the TV news and thought, "Hey, I feel so chilled now!" Or when did you come off Facebook feeling like a more whole and centred human being? Let me guess. Never? Yeah, me neither.

The fact is that when we plug ourselves into such media, we are opening up our minds to a deluge of influences from marketeers, manipulators and strategists who want to stir up your emotions and manipulate them to get an outcome, whether it's buying a product, voting for a certain party, liking a page, or following their YouTube channel. The more toxic media manipulators will try to influence your thinking by stirring up your sense of outrage, sending your emotional mind into a frenzy and then the thought-bombs start exploding all over the place. It's small wonder that we all get so stressed if we expose ourselves to these influences voluntarily.

But you can try something much more pleasant. Take your senses for a walk and open yourself to Active Awareness. You can use it for pleasure when life is calm, and when life gets difficult, you can switch to being actively engaged with the moment to manage stress.

It's my gift to you today.

The Kiwi Vine.

I once lived in a house that had a vast Kiwi vine growing along one side. The leaves on a Kiwi are wide, so you could barely see the wall underneath. It was an impressive plant.

Then winter came. I happened to be watching as the garden thermometer showed the temperature was falling towards freezing for the first time that year. The moment it fell exactly to freezing-point, a remarkable thing happened. All the leaves on the Kiwi spontaneously dropped. Within minutes, the whole of the huge vine was bare and its leaves carpeted the ground.

I mention this because I think something similar happens with our emotions and our moods.

Sometimes an event external to ourselves happens that throws us into turmoil, such as someone's outrageous behaviour or injustice, and our mood changes in an instant. This is made worse if we are powerless to change what has happened and forceful emotions like resentment, rage, regret and frustration rob us of our peace of mind.

Other times, though, our emotions change for reasons we cannot see and our mood falls as dramatically as the leaves of the Kiwi when the temperature hit freezing. If you don't know the cause, this is bewildering, even frightening. Possibly your emotional mind had picked up a trigger for an emotional response that you had missed with your conscious logical mind, or maybe there had been a hormonal change in your body. You may never know the cause.

You might think that you are lacking in some way, you might be ashamed, you might turn to prescription meds or recreational drugs to improve your mood, or act out behaviours that bring you relief. But these solutions often create even greater difficulties.

A few years ago, I was living in a lovely village, in a great relationship, with stimulating work to do, life was on the up. Then as the winter arrived, suddenly one day my mood dropped like those Kiwi leaves. Out of nowhere, depression hit me. I felt desperate, life didn't seem worth living. As I had no history of depression, this was doubly surprising.

My doctor said I had *Seasonally Adjusted Disorder*, a type of depression triggered by falling light levels in winter. I had never liked the dark days of winter, but it had never hit me like this before. He wrote me a prescription for Citalopram, told me to get a lightbox, and encouraged me to buck up.

I'm not used to taking prescription meds, and the Citalopram made me feel like throwing myself under one of the buses that passed our house. I soon ditched them. I couldn't take a lightbox around with me all day, so that was a limited remedy.

As I'm CBT-trained, I could use cognitive therapy on myself, which helped. I constantly reminded myself that nothing was wrong and that it would pass. But I still felt wretched and the sun stubbornly refused to emerge from the clouds. There had to be another solution.

I was working in an addictions therapy project and, as luck would have it, we were taught about using mindfulness to help clients. Although mindfulness was getting a lot of publicity at the time, I knew very little about it. I guess I had just dismissed it as a fad. But when I learned about the science behind it, I was impressed.

Mindfulness, as we know it in the West, originated in the Massachusetts Medical School in the 1980s as a treatment for stress. Neuroscientists can show how mindfulness lights up the brain, so you don't have to take a leap of faith that this works, you can actually see it working on brain scans. The health service in the UK is particularly keen on mindfulness, recommending that it's at least as effective as medication to relieve anxiety. Research shows that it reduces the chance of a recurrence of depression by 50%. But unlike meds, which invariably have undesirable side effects, the most common side effect of mindfulness is increased happiness.

I threw myself into mindfulness, attending groups and practising alone twice daily. It worked. It wasn't a miracle cure. The depression was still there, but it was manageable. If I was having a bad day, I would excuse myself from work for a few minutes and use a brief mindfulness practice standing outside the office. I had an emergency go-to practice for such occasions, like the one you have already learned about in the chapter *Dynamic De-stress*. It got me through the winter and then one day in the Spring, the sun came out and my depression lifted as suddenly as it arrived.

Since then, I have been involved in running mindfulness courses for clients and have seen first-hand how it changes people's emotional landscape for the better. The main obstacle many people have to overcome in trying it is the notion that mindfulness is somehow out-there and woo-woo. But science shows that it isn't like that at all. It helps you see how your thinking works, and as we have seen already in this book, it's your thinking that sparks your emotional responses. I don't use it every day now. But it's always there as my place of safety when life gets stressy.

Many mindfulness practices exist. In the next chapter, I will share one with you that I have found particularly effective.

Clouds.

When you read the chapter about Active Awareness, you were, in fact, reading about how to apply the concept of mindfulness to your world. Today, we will look at how to use mindfulness in a more formal way to take away stress and anxiety, making you feel more emotionally balanced.

The mindful practice I will present in this chapter is a versatile all-rounder. I've used it myself countless times. It helps to ground yourself at the start of the day. It helps you sleep at the end of the day. It can be helpful at any time.

I want you to try this today, then every day for the rest of this 10-day program. Don't skip this. It's important. Not only will this practice help you feel better, but it will also, over time, retrain your brain to see your life in a more helpful and positive way. Repeating this practice is key. The more you do, the quicker and better will be the results.

You will need to ring-fence around 10 minutes each day to carry this out. If you think that it will be difficult to find the time because you are too busy, then it's even more important to make the time. This is vital for your welfare.

Not prioritizing your wellbeing is a sign of stress. By putting yourself first, you will start to relieve that stress.

This is your special time. For the next few minutes, I want you to park your worries and feelings that you need to do something else, or that you need to be somewhere else. In these few minutes, you can let all that go without feeling guilty. Whatever you have to cope with, you will do better after having this special time. Or maybe you will realize that you can let go forever of these things that trouble you.

I want you to think of your time to meditate as being a place of comfort you can go to whenever life gets too much, or whenever you just want to enjoy some space in your head. This time is a place of tranquillity and warmth that is always there for you when you need it.

Read through the instructions below. You don't need to memorize it. To help you, we have made a recording you can listen to, details of which are at the end of the chapter.

Mindfulness is different from the relaxation audios you have used already. With those, the object was simply to relax and it didn't matter if you just let it wash over you and didn't listen closely. Mindfulness is a form of mental training and as such, you need to be attentive to get the best from it. That's why I don't recommend using a recliner or a bed as you might fall asleep. If you should fall asleep, don't worry, though. You must have needed a nap, and you can try the mindfulness another time.

To begin, you will need to be somewhere you will be undisturbed. If you are at home and there are other people around, tell them you need 15 minutes alone (or longer, if you wish) so you can study this book. Explain it's important and ask for their support.

Your mindfulness place should feel comfortable and warm. Remember, your emotional mind will be monitoring what you're doing, so if it feels reassured, it will send out contented feelings. You will need an upright chair, not a recliner, or a thick rug or couch if you want to lie down.

The intention is to feel relaxed and comfortable, but alert. If you are feeling stressed or anxious, it would be a good idea to spend a couple of minutes doing the Dynamic De-stress before you start the meditation.

When you are ready, make yourself comfortable on the chair or rug. If you are sitting, your back should be upright but relaxed, your feet flat on the floor, your hands on your lap in whatever way feels comfortable, and your weight evenly distributed on the seat. If you are lying down, your legs should be slightly apart, your arms a few inches away from your sides with your palms facing up, and your spine straight.

Take a few moments to explore the sensations of where your body is in contact with the surface below you. If you are seated, pay particular attention to your feet and the contact they are making with the ground or the inside of your shoes. If you are lying down, feel all the points where your body is in direct contact with the surface below. You don't need to think about it, just feel what it's like.

Next, allow your body to feel loose and heavy and let it sink into the surface below. Don't force it, just let gravity gently pull your weight downwards. Take a few moments to enjoy the sensations of looseness. Allow your eyes to close, or soften your gaze.

Now turn your attention to the sensation of hearing. Tune in to the sounds in the world around you. Notice the pitch of the sounds and which ones are close and which are distant. Notice how sounds come and go, which are in the room and which are outside. Take a few moments to explore all these sounds. You don't need to think about them, just experience them. If you find that you have started to think about a sound and your mind has become caught up in a train of thought, refocus on exploring all the sounds in your world at that moment.

When you feel ready to move on, allow the sounds to fade and move your attention inside your body to the sound of your breathing. How is that today? Is it slow and rhythmical, or fast and shallow? Don't try to change it, simply observe what you find. Notice the subtle differences, no two breaths are quite the same. Notice the sensation of the air moving as it flows in and out past the tip of your nose.

When you realize a thought has distracted you from observing your breathing, note what the thought is. Maybe it's worry or planning or a memory from the past. Whatever it is, imagine it turns into a cloud, watch it float away on the breeze, or vaporize if you prefer, and then return to observing your breathing. Every time you realize you have been caught up in a thought, do the same: note what the thought is about, imagine it turn into a cloud and float away. Watch it go until it's out of sight then return to your breathing.

Continue this for as long as you feel able. If you have never meditated before, this might only be a couple of minutes. If you are experienced, it might be half an hour. You decide what is right for you. But do not stop because you feel rushed. Remember, stressed people feel rushed, and if you behave like a stressed person, you will be one.

Finally, when you're ready, turn your attention out from yourself and connect with the sounds in your environment. Then gradually open your eyes, take a stretch, and you're ready to get on with your day.

Reflect on being able to turn your worries, plans and memories into clouds and watch them float away or vaporize.

How did that feel?

If you are inexperienced in using mindfulness, you might find it easier to listen to a guided meditation. With this in mind, meditation teacher Antonia Ryan has written a mindfulness meditation, based on Clouds, and recorded it for you.

The mp3 is on the same webpage as the Deep Relaxation audios you have already used. Here is the link again: www.subscribepage.com/emotions_audio. When you have logged in, you will see a link to the mp3 audio downloads page. You will also get an email from me that gives you a link to the audios. (If you cannot get your audios with either of the above methods, send me an email to emotions.downloads@gmail.com and an autoresponder will email you back with an alternative link immediately.)

We have taken a deep dive into mindfulness today. I recommend you keep practising, as the separation it gives you from your emotional side is a key skill if you can master it. You may find the formal kind of meditation in Clouds works for you, or you might have preferred the more active kind of mindfulness in Active Awareness. Either way, you will benefit.

Over the last few days, we have looked at concepts and techniques you can employ to keep yourself emotionally balanced and reduce stress and anxiety. Over the next few days, we will be focusing on situations that commonly cause people emotional upset and what to do about them when they crop up in your life.

Day Five.

Approval.

When you were a small child, your emotional side ran the show. Your logical mind takes years to develop, but your emotional mind comes out of the womb fired up and ready to go.

It analyses all the input from this new world you have entered and feeds it back to you in thoughts and feelings that you instinctively respond to. When it doesn't find everything to its liking, it tells you to cry, and you cry. If it tells you to scream, you scream. It will be years before your logical mind gives you the ability to override your emotional brain's commands.

Your emotional mind has a great set of tools to control you: neurotransmitters. These are the brain's feel-good chemicals. There are various neurotransmitters, and I could fill up pages discussing them. But this is a book about feeling better in 10 days. It's about results. So I'm going to keep the neuroscience to the point. For the purposes of this book, we're interested in adrenaline, which is associated with stress; serotonin, which is associated with wellbeing;

and dopamine, which is associated with short-term gratification.

As a small child, gratification is what we're all about. We don't think about what others want. We want food, shelter, company and sleep. These are our must-have essentials. But then, pretty soon as we develop, our list of essentials lengthens. Early on, we discover something else that is important. We know it's important because our emotional mind rewards us with a shot of lovely dopamine when we get it: approval.

Think of a toddler playing with its mother. It wants praise. If it doesn't get it or if it gets told off, it will cry. No approval, no dopamine, boo-hoo! Pretty soon, the little one develops strategies to get approval. It will learn that if it does certain cute things, it gets approval. It also learns that if the approval isn't forthcoming, then it has a big nuclear button it can press - screaming the house down. Or even better, screaming and going bright red in a public place until the parent gives in and starts placating the child with soothing, approving words. Finally, the child's emotional mind is pacified and the tantrum stops.

As we grow up, our desire for praise widens to include teachers, school friends, co-workers, employers, intimate partners and so on. Approval becomes an important part of social interaction. Since the arrival of social media, this has even grown to include friends we have never met. Facebook has become a multi-billion-dollar business on the back of our desire for approval. Its "thumbs-up" symbol screams approval.

So, is there a problem with this? Surely, it's only human nature to be liked, isn't it? Well, sure, anyone would prefer to be liked. But there is a massive problem:

The desire for approval puts our happiness in the hands of other people.

Approval is only one side of the coin. The other side is rejection and emotional pain. If your happiness relies on what you believe other people think of you, on how many likes your selfie gets on Facebook, on whether that guy you fancy asks you out, then you are wide open to being emotionally crushed. Sooner or later you will suffer rejection and the pain-birds will fly into your life.

Imagine, for instance, you are a needy office worker. Your day revolves around approval, especially from your manager. On your way into work one morning, you have what you think is a brilliant idea for a new service your company could offer to its customers. "Wow", you think, "the boss is gonna love this." By the time you reach the office, you have convinced yourself you have the best idea ever, and you are already envisioning your promotion and raise, and your boss presenting you as the employee of the year at the company's annual convention. You're bubbling inside with excitement; you can almost taste that big dose of dopamine that comes with praise.

You give up your lunch break to put your idea down in an email to your manager. You read your email through a couple of times. You decide it's a masterpiece. The company cannot fail to be impressed by your genius. You address it to you manager and hit *send*. The snag is that you just sent your emotional wellbeing off with that email and put it in the hands of someone else.

Throughout the afternoon, you keep an eye on your inbox, waiting for the response from your boss, which you expect to be gushing with praise for your brilliance. You are so excited you can hardly breathe. But the emails that come in are just the routine messages copied to everyone in the department. As the afternoon wears on, worry starts to replace your excitement. By home-time, there is no response.

That night, you hardly sleep. You're beating yourself up, wondering why you sent that damned email. On the way to work the next day, your mind is racing. You're still holding on to the hope that the boss will be there to celebrate your genius and reward you with praise, but the churning in your stomach and the light-headedness you are experiencing tells you something is wrong. You start fearing the worst. What if you have made some huge error? What if they're going to laugh at you. Now you're imagining the boss is already in the office, telling everyone what a dork you are. You race into the office, heart racing, hands shaking. All is quiet. You check your emails, still no response. You cannot stand it anymore. You knock on the manager's door and put your head around. "Oh hi," you say, trying to be nonchalant. "I just wondered if you saw my email yesterday?"

"Oh yes," comes the reply. "Thanks for that, but we tried something similar a few years ago, and it didn't work."

You are crushed. You return to your desk feeling your life is over. You want to run away and cry. Later that day, bitterness sets in and you are telling anyone who will listen that the manager is a moron.

In fact, the manager is blameless. Our imaginary office worker has gone through hours of self-inflicted emotional torment for no reason other than to get a moment of praise. Although this is a story, I have seen people acting-out like this in every place I've worked. And it's not restricted to work, people are constantly trying to feed their hunger for approval in every aspect of their lives.

We all do this to some extent. Indeed, the exchange of praise (or lack of it) is an important part of human interaction, it's feedback. It shows us where we stand in relationships, how we are doing at work or if we are treating people as they want to be treated. But if approval-seeking gets out of hand and you spend your time people-pleasing to get it, then, at some point, it's going to bite you on your emotional backside, as with our office worker.

Approval-seeking behaviour is in direct relation to your feelings of self-worth. If you have low self-worth, your need for approval will be high, and vice-versa. Low self-worth comes from three main areas:

- Criticism. If you were often harshly criticized as a child, you are likely to have grown up with low self-worth. This can also happen later in life, especially if you find yourself in a relationship where you are openly criticized. You will seek approval to help you feel better about yourself. The solution is to take responsibility for your self-worth. This takes the power away from others.

- Vulnerability. If you feel you are in a vulnerable situation - maybe because you rely on others for help or you lack money - you are likely to people-please. This reduces your self-worth because you see others in an elevated position of power over you. People-pleasing keeps you vulnerable. The solution is to take action on the core reason for your vulnerability.

- Competence. If you feel you are out of your depth in a situation, your self-worth may suffer. It might be that you need help to build your competency in an area. You may feel that you are lacking as a person in some way when, really, you need to learn a skill so that your feeling of competence is restored.

If you find you are caught in a pattern of people-pleasing to gain approval, there is an exercise I want you to try in order to break out. Today, I want you to look for an opportunity to do something beneficial for someone else without them knowing. Do not tell anyone what you have done. Do not look for praise. Simply do whatever it is, then get on with your day.

So if, let's say, you're at work and you notice a colleague has made an error that you can rectify, then do it. Don't call your colleague and point out the error, and don't put it right and go looking for praise. Just do it and move on. You can feel satisfaction, that's great, but have it come from inside you rather than from someone else. If you are at home and you realize your partner has forgotten to do a household chore task, then do it yourself. When your partner gets home, don't point out what you have done, don't go looking for praise. I want you to do this exercise every day for the rest of the 10 days.

If you are used to people-pleasing, this might feel strange at first, but you are telling your emotional brain that you don't need someone else to make you feel good. You start to build self-worth. You might not get that same nice dopamine feeling you have when you get direct praise, but over time, as you increasingly feel good about yourself without praise, you will have another neurotransmitter kick in – serotonin. This is generated when you do something well, when you give of yourself, rather than when someone gives to you, and serotonin gives a long-term feeling of wellbeing and satisfaction. If you happen to receive praise as well, regard that as a bonus, not a necessity.

I often recommend to clients who are going through a difficult time emotionally that they look for opportunities to help other people. The clients usually don't see the point at first. Because they have problems, they think the spotlight should be on them. But by moving the spotlight to what you can do for others, you do yourself a favour. You break the cycle of rumination and being locked in your head, you build your self-esteem, and get a mental bath in serotonin, all of which is sure to elevate your mood.

Assumptions.

I had just finished running my regular Tuesday morning therapeutic group when one of the attendees, Shannon, said: "Can I have a word?" You always know that means trouble.

"Can I switch to attending the group on another day?"

"You could come in on Fridays, if you like," I said. "Why, what's the problem?"

"It's Andrea," Shannon replied. "She's really upsetting me."

That confused me. There had been about a dozen people at the group. Andrea had been sitting opposite Shannon, but as far as I could recall, Andrea hadn't said a great deal, so I didn't know how she could have bothered Shannon.

"How's she upset you?"

"Oh, it's the way she looks at me. She was doing it all through the meeting. I know she looks down on me, just because I'm not posh like her."

"Did she say anything to you?" I asked.

"No, she didn't need to. It's that look on her face. We talk in the group about being non-judgmental, but she just sits there judging me all the time."

I commented that Andrea probably couldn't help looking at Shannon, as she was opposite her, but Shannon was having none of it and headed to the exit.

Two minutes later I happened to look out the window and saw the group members leaving the building and walking down the street. To my amazement, Shannon and Andrea were chatting away like old friends, all smiles.

By chance, the following day I was due to see Shannon for a one-to-one meeting. I had to ask what had happened.

"Oh, that!" said Shannon. "Well, just after I left, Andrea came over to me and said what a lovely scarf I was wearing."

"So, she hadn't been judging you during the group, she'd been admiring your scarf?" I asked.

"Yes."

"So you two are all right with each other?"

"Yes, we went for a coffee after. She's really nice when you get to know her."

I recount this little story to illustrate a point. If you make assumptions, you can be widely off target. It happens all the time. We see someone and from the look on their face, we instantly assume we know what they're thinking.

Assumptions come from a curious belief that we have supernatural or God-like powers. It might come as a surprise to you to discover that you can think this way, but you do – at times, we all do. In Shannon's case, she didn't question that she was acting like a clairvoyant. Yet if I had suggested that she was behaving like a psychic, she would probably have thought I was crazy. Nevertheless, she assumed that she could read Andrea's mind. In fact, she was guessing, but she was convinced that she was right. This had led to Shannon becoming upset at Andrea for what she assumed was Andrea's negative view of her. So Shannon sat through the meeting, her sense of outrage with Andrea growing, while Andrea was simply admiring Shannon's scarf.

As it turned out, the situation was defused after the meeting when Andrea made a kind comment about the scarf. But imagine what would have happened if that conversation had not taken place. Shannon would have gone home in a mood. She might have lost sleep because of a sense of outrage. She would have changed her diary to avoid coming to the groups that Andrea attended. She might have had a simmering resentment for weeks, maybe longer. Shannon could have brought emotional pain on herself, and all because of something that had never happened.

In the case of Shannon and Andrea, no damage was done. But mistaken mind-reading causes havoc in intimate, family and business relationships. If you think that, say, your partner is in a bad mood, you might react in a way that starts an argument, when in reality your partner was merely daydreaming and can't understand why you've jumped off the deep end. The result is emotional pain for both of you.

The reverse of this is also problematic. This is where you assume that someone knows what you are thinking.

Because of this assumption, you expect the other person to behave in a certain way. Let's say, you have just come home from work, it's been a difficult day and you're tired. Although you said you would make dinner, you would really like your partner to do it. You assume your partner will see you're tired and volunteer to cook. He doesn't. You get cross because you're frustrated he hasn't reacted as you wanted. You might go into a mood and sulk. He gets angry at you because he doesn't know what he's done to provoke your moody behaviour. Again, the result is self-inflicted emotional pain.

Today, I would like you to look out for assumptions cropping up in your own thinking. If you can spot them, you can save yourself from totally unnecessary emotional pain. Question your assumption.

- Does your assumption stand up to scrutiny, or are you behaving like a psychic?
- Does your assumption say more about you, rather than the other person? In Shannon's case, she thought Andrea was looking down on her. Does this indicate Shannon has an issue with her own sense of self-worth, which had nothing to do with Andrea?
- Have you expressed yourself clearly in a situation, or are you assuming that the other person knows

something they might not be aware of? In other words, are you creating your own problem?
- If the other person has not verbally confirmed what you believe, would asking for clarification help?
- In written communications like text messages, social media posts and emails, have you misinterpreted the tone? It's easily done, which is why emoticons have become popular to clarify the meaning behind the words. But even these can be misinterpreted.
- If your assumption is right, does it matter? For instance, if you assume that someone at work doesn't like you, based on their body language, you could be wrong or right. But if you are right, is that really an issue? No matter how wonderful you are, there will always be someone who doesn't like you.

Everyday life can throw up enough emotionally challenging situations without creating ones of your own. Today we have looked at some you can avoid for yourself. Tomorrow, we get stuck into some really useful insights to keep the pain-birds out of your world.

Day Six.

Anger.

Bradley burst into my consulting room without making eye-contact, dropped onto the seat with a thud, and looked at the floor. His posture was textbook negativity.

"What's up, Brad?" I asked.

"I'm so hacked off." He said, still looking at the floor. "It's like everywhere I go people just want to get under my skin. It's not fair. Then something happens and everyone blames me."

"So what has happened?"

"I just had a big argument at the truck hire place. I needed a vehicle to take some stuff up north. Anyway, I gave them my bank card and they said they could only accept a credit card. I said that I would pay in cash. How reasonable is that? But they said they still needed the credit card for the fuel deposit."

"You don't have a credit card?"

"It's maxed out. I couldn't give them that," he said, looking up for the first time. "I said, couldn't they make an exception as they know me? But they said it was company rules. So there I was, with a load of stuff to get to Manchester by this evening, they had a truck they could have let me have there-and-then, but no. Anyway, I lost it."

"You lost it? You mean you lost your temper?"

"Yeah, you know me. I went into one. I started shouting. I knocked their credit card machine on the floor. They threatened to call the police, so I left. Now I'm in a right mess. Those people and their stupid rules. Why couldn't they just take my debit card? It's an outrageous way to run a business."

I had met Bradley a few times. He had come to me about an addiction problem, but it had become clear that his addiction was his way of trying to medicate his frustration and anger issues. He believed the world was against him. He thought that people behaved outrageously and didn't treat him with the respect he thought he deserved. He felt frustrated and angry most of the time. His emotional brain was constantly on the lookout for examples of new outrages against him, and when it saw one, it would fire out a thought-bomb and he always reacted with anger.

Bradley believed that the source of his frustration with the world was other people's outrageous behaviour towards him. He used the word 'outrageous' frequently. His way of dealing with this was turning his anger on the world in the forlorn hope that one day the world would see the error of its ways and treat him better. Of course, this never happened and he became more frustrated, resentful and angrier. Bradley was turning into a raging bull of toxic emotions. As a result of his short temper, he already had a record for criminal damage, and I feared that one day it would boil over, leading to a more serious offence.

Looking from the outside, it was clear that the source of Bradley's frustrations was not caused by the outside world, but by his own beliefs. He thought that everyone should treat him better and agree to his view of the world, but if you asked Bradley why he believed that, he could not answer. He assumed that his thoughts were facts, as most people do. But thoughts are not facts, they are merely thoughts. Bradley's world would never be the way he thought it should be.

The problem lay in the gap between his expectations and reality. That gap was where all his resentments and frustrations came from. Bradley was trying to close that gap by forcing the world to change, but in doing that, he was attempting something outside his control. What he could not see was that the gap could be closed in an instant if he changed his expectations, which were entirely within his power.

On that particular day, Bradley's anger was at the rental company not wanting to change their hire rules to suit him. He saw their rules as being the problem, not his maxed-out credit card, so in his mind, this was more evidence of the world being against him. Bradley's emotional brain had filtered out the truth that Bradley was responsible for his credit card, rather than the rental company.

His emotional brain shielded him from this truth because it was easier for him to blame someone else for his shortcomings than take responsibility for them. But by not taking responsibility, he lost control.

When you think about it, in Bradley's case, it makes much more sense for him to accept that the world is not always fair and will not do what he wants, rather than fight a painful war for control with the world. In life, it pays to fight the battles you can win, rather than get beaten up all the time, even if that means you have to accept that you can be wrong sometimes. Nevertheless, Bradley went to war with life every day and got a beating every day.

Attempting to change what is outside your control is one of the great sources of stress and emotional pain.

Bradley's anger issues were resolvable, but first, it was necessary to find a way to help him insert that vital moment for reflection when an emotional trigger thought-bombed him. When anger is provoked, it escalates quickly, and if you don't do something fast, the neural pathway from the logical brain to the emotional brain gets shut down temporarily, and pure emotion – rage – takes over. It's the moment that some people call the "red mist" rising, then anything can happen.

Bradley could have benefitted from mindful training, but I had already discussed that with him, and his mind was closed to it. He was convinced, for no reason, that it was 'some sort of hippy thing'. I needed a way to help his thinking that would appeal to him. I tried using a version of the Scale of Ten.

"Tell me, Brad. What are you going to do after you leave here?"

"Probably go to the pub, I expect," he said. "You never know, maybe I'll meet someone there I can sell my stuff to."

"Brad, would you be willing to try a smart thinking exercise?"

For the first time in the session, he looked engaged. "Smart thinking? How's that work?" While mindfulness didn't fit with his image of himself, smart thinking was different. It appealed to his ego.

"Let's think about your situation," I said. "You have a customer in Manchester. You have goods for him here. You need a vehicle. You have no credit on your card. Those are the facts?"

He nodded.

"So, think about what happened this morning, when you lost your temper at the rental company. On a scale of one to ten, where ten would be really likely and one would be totally unlikely, how would you score losing your temper in terms of sorting out the situation?"

"Oh, I don't know, maybe a three. They might have changed their minds," he replied, but without conviction.

"Okay, so how likely is it, on a scale of one to ten, that you will find someone at the pub who will buy your goods?"

He looked doubtful. "Probably one."

"Now score this," I said. "If you contacted your customer in Manchester and asked to deliver tomorrow, then rang around other hire companies to find one that would accept your debit card, how likely is that to work, out of ten?"

He looked animated. "Maybe six or seven. I guess it's worth a shot."

With that, we ended the session. He had phone calls to make.

Over the next couple of sessions, we worked on using the Scale of Ten as a way to diffuse his short temper. The logic was that when he felt anger rising in a situation, that he should pause, look at his options, scale them, and act on the highest scoring option.

This was against his default way of reacting that he had learned in childhood and had reinforced every time since. But Bradley could see that this would turn him into a winner, rather than a fighter who got continually beaten up. He learned how to use Dynamic De-stress to defuse his anger. This kept the neural pathway to his logical mind open, so he could rationally use scaling.

He found that he could use this in all his relationships, not just in business. Over time, this led to less stress and anxiety in his life because he was carrying out fewer anger-based actions. These are usually self-defeating because they result in unplanned repercussions, like legal or relationship difficulties. It improved his world view because he no longer felt the world was against him. He saw that if he took actions that were based on a rational scaling system, rather than 'gut feel', the world treated him better.

Today, I want you to be on the alert for anger. You might not be as destructive as Bradley, but we all have anger to some extent. The repercussions of anger are usually self-sabotaging and that will have a negative impact on your emotional state and general feeling of wellbeing. When you feel anger rising, remember to step back, use Dynamic De-stress if necessary, and scale your options. Go with the option that gives you the highest score.

This takes practice. Overcoming a default emotional reaction takes time. But if you continually scale your options and go with the one that scores the highest, even if it goes against your gut feeling, you will inevitably become more of a winner in life, have better days, become more confident, and you will enjoy more positive emotions.

Bradley's angry outbursts were examples of rage, a short-term explosion of anger. But there is another version of anger which differs in that it's long-term and can be even more toxic: resentment.

We'll look at that next.

Resentment.

Not all of us suffer from rage. But it would be an unusual person who had no resentments. It could be argued that resentments are more harmful to our emotional balance. Rage is over quickly. If you do no lasting damage during an outburst, you can move on from it. But resentments last a long time, we often carry resentments that begin in childhood until we die. Resentment is a chronic form of anger.

Resentments have their origins either in injustice or jealousy, and we justify our negative feelings through the argument that life should be fair.

A new resentment based on injustice is second only to having a major loss in the amount of emotional damage it causes. It keeps you awake at night, it gnaws at you when you get up, it follows you around and won't let you get peace of mind. It feels like the pain-birds are picking over your bones. Over time, the anguish might ease but, untreated, it never goes away and years after the trigger event, it can come back to churn up your feelings.

When you are on the receiving end of apparent injustice, you feel the burning emotion of outrage, leading to resentment. You feel you have been dealt with unfairly. If you have been treated badly, maybe you need to express anger or outrage as the start of returning to emotional balance. But if you hold on to that sense of outrage over time and it becomes a resentment, all you achieve is prolonged anguish.

Often, the person suffering the resentment feels the pain while the other person carries on oblivious. For instance, if you lose your cool because the call centre at your bank is giving you the run-around when you want to sort out a problem, slamming down the phone on an unhelpful employee might leave you with a resentment that eats at you for days, but the employee will move on and forget you existed. This shows the futility of holding onto resentments. You want the other person to suffer, but you are the one who feels the pain.

The urge for revenge usually accompanies resentments. But while revenge might appeal to your base instincts (which is why revenge-based movies achieve good box-office sales) it is unlikely to help your emotional wellbeing. Dreaming about revenge if you are not going to act is a waste of your valuable life and will only stir up more painful feelings.

Some people carry resentments with them for decades and all the time dream of revenge. But if you act on a plan for revenge, you are opening up the prospect of a volatile situation and an eruption of new issues and resentments in its aftermath.

Consequently, most advice you read about resentments talks about letting go. This would seem to be good advice. If you let go of the resentment, you let go of those toxic emotions that it engenders, so you will feel better. Sounds great. But there's one little problem with the usual advice to let go: it's hard to do because it feels so unfair. So, if you try to let go, your emotional brain will behave like a petulant toddler who has just been told to eat broccoli instead of chocolate. It's going to throw its metaphorical arms in the air, stamp its feet and scream the house down – and the house is your head.

If your logical mind is going to get the upper hand and allow you to let go of your pain, it will need a strategy. So, let's look at your resentments. I want you to think of a resentment you have in your life. It could be about something that's still happening, or maybe something from your past that you cannot let it go, so it still hurts.

Next, I want you to look at this resentment through the lens of total honesty. When you have a resentment, you feel 100% convinced that you are the victim, you think you have the moral high ground, and that the other party deserves to die a long and painful death. But is that true?

Sure, it can happen that you really are the victim. For instance, if you were unlucky enough to be on the receiving end of an act of random violence from a stranger, then nobody would dispute that you are the victim with the moral high ground. But most times, resentments aren't like that. If you are totally honest with yourself, you see that at least some of what has happened is down to you.

Going back to Bradley's story, we can see how resentment can start. His initial rage at the rental company declining his payment method could easily turn into a long-term resentment against that particular company. If he had followed his default way of thinking, he would have been bad-mouthing the company for years to anyone willing to listen. He might even have acted out a revenge scenario, like putting a brick through the company's window one night when he was drunk. But would that have been justified? No. It was not the rental company's problem that Bradley had spent out on his credit card. And Bradley's dislike at the company's hire rules was because they didn't suit him, not because they were wrong. If Bradley had a valid credit card, he wouldn't have cared less about their rules because they would have suited him. Bradley himself had a massive hand in what happened and he would have been entirely responsible for any ensuing resentment.

Looking at your resentment, can you 100% say you were totally blameless? It's hard to admit to yourself any blame, especially in a long-running resentment, but if you can, it will help your emotional mind calm down. If you see that you were at least partly at fault, then it takes the heat out of emotions. It can be a first step to letting go.

So if you resent your ex-partner for walking out on you, are you certain that you never did anything to contribute to the break-up? Was is totally the other person's fault? Are you being honest with yourself? If you resent your school for the poor grades you got, are you sure it was their poor teaching that was to blame? Did you really put total effort into your homework? If you resent your boss for not giving you a promotion, are you sure it wasn't because you weren't the best candidate?

Isn't it time to acknowledge that you had a hand in causing the situation that led to the resentment and let it go? You don't need to start beating yourself up, as that will open up a new avenue of emotional pain. Simply look at what you can learn from the situation and say goodbye to that resentment you've been holding onto like some family heirloom. Letting go is not a defeat, it's a relief. When you let it go, you also let go of the pain it's causing you.

If you drill down further into your resentment, you will likely find it's based on the idea that life should be fair and you have been treated unfairly. This sounds like a valid justification for your resentment because we are brought up to believe that fairness is a good thing. We don't question that. But does that stack up when looked at through the lens of total honesty?

What you believe is fair will not necessarily be the same as someone else. We all have our own interpretation of what fair means. So when you think that life is unfair, what you are really saying is that life is not how you think it should be. That's a different thing. When you say you are being treated unfairly, you are saying you are not being treated as you believe you should be. It's your ego that's causing the resentment. You aren't getting what you want, and that hurts. Your emotional mind fires out thought-bombs, telling you it's outrageous that you cannot have what you want and that someone should be blamed. So you start a resentment and the next thing you know, you are awake half the night because of the torment it's causing you.

It's the same with resentments based on jealousy. You think it's unfair that someone else has something you don't. But that's because you believe you are entitled to whatever it is you are jealous of. Are you sure about that? Or is it another case of not having what you want?

But how about if your resentment is one of the minority of instances where you really are 100% the victim of someone's terrible behaviour? Surely you're justified in having a resentment then, aren't you? Well, maybe you are. But if you have been seriously wronged, you would still be better trying to let go, even though that might seem totally unjust. Why? Because while you have that resentment causing you distress, you are letting the person who caused your pain to continue hurting you. You might not have been responsible for the event that caused the original pain, but you can take responsibility for the ongoing resentment and the pain it's causing you now.

You can make a start today by using the 'Clouds' meditation. Every time your resentment comes to mind, imagine it floating away. If you are dealing with a severe wrong-doing, you might need one-to-one counselling as well as the support of this book, in which case, make a start and book yourself a session with a counsellor today.

Taking control of your resentments means that you take responsibility for them. This might seem unfair, but this is another way you can empower yourself by taking your emotional wellbeing out of the hands of other people. That has to be good.

Day Seven.

Addictive Behaviours.

When negative emotions cause you to experience low mood, it's tempting to look for a quick fix – something you can take to change that mood. Consequently, many people turn to medications, alcohol and recreational drugs to feel okay again. After all, why go to all the bother of doing all that psychological stuff, when you can just pour yourself a scotch, light up a spliff, or swallow a pill?

This can work in the short-term. If you take a depressant, it will sedate you, which can feel pleasant if your head has been whizzing around like a spin-dryer. Common depressant drugs include marijuana, alcohol, opioid painkillers like Codeine, and benzodiazepine medications like Valium or Xanax.

What's more, you get an extra reward – your brain releases dopamine, the natural feel-good chemical. Now, doesn't that feel better? Probably it will, at least for a few minutes.

Stimulant drugs, like caffeine, nicotine, cocaine and amphetamines, obviously won't have the same sedating effect as depressants, quite the opposite. But they also cause that dopamine release, which is the common link with all these varying substances. So it might seem that using them is a good idea, as they turn your mood quickly.

However, there is a problem – rebound.

The Law of Rebound states that any drug will have the opposite effect when it wears off. This means that whatever mood you were trying to escape from will come hurtling back into your life, often much worse than it was before.

Take nicotine. If you have been a regular smoker, you will know that if you have been unable to smoke for a while, your concentration wavers, and if you have to go an extended time without smoking, you start to feel like you're losing your mind. It comes as a great relief when you light up. For a short time, you will feel restored to sanity because the nicotine withdrawal quickly subsides and you feel good. But within minutes of finishing smoking, the nicotine starts leaving your system and rebound sets in. An hour later, you will be back to where you started.

Caffeine, if you drink a lot of it, can have a similar effect. As with nicotine, rebound sets in quickly. If you are a light coffee drinker, this is not much of a problem. You might get a small craving, nothing more. But frequent drinkers of strong coffee will feel their concentration faltering and might even start to get the shakes if they go too long without a caffeine fix.

While I know the effects of nicotine and caffeine from personal experience, I've never taken crack cocaine, but I've worked with many people who have. I'm told it feels amazing. It sends your dopamine levels through the roof and into orbit. But only for a few minutes. Then your dopamine levels come crashing down and so does your mood. It certainly elevates your mood fast, but the rebound is nasty.

Marijuana will help you relax and your cares might drift away, for a while at least. But rebound can set in while you are still stoned, and marijuana is notorious for causing paranoia, taking away your peace of mind and making things worse.

With alcohol, the rebound effect can set in after just a couple of drinks. Alcohol has an unfortunate side-effect if you are in emotional pain, as it exaggerates your underlying emotions. So, if you were angry before you had a drink, after that initial hit of dopamine has worn off, you might be worse than ever, in total fury. If you were feeling sad before you had a drink, after rebound starts to kick in, you could be feeling desperate.

If you are taking a prescribed drug, you will not experience rebound if you take it regularly, in accordance with your doctor's advice. But you are saving up the rebound effect for the day you come off it. I have met many people in my work who have been on a prescription for years and are terrified of coming off, in fear of the rebound. I'm not suggesting you should ignore your doctor if you are prescribed a drug. You might need it. But I think that as a culture we accept that reaching out for a drug is appropriate when an emotional difficulty comes along, rather than as a last resort.

So because of rebound, taking a substance to help your mood is entirely counterproductive. And there's more bad news. Unlike the safe methods for dealing with emotional pain which I describe in this book, taking a substance has side-effects. The severity tends to be dose-responsive, so the more you take, the bigger the side-effect. I have lost count of the people I have seen lose jobs, lose relationships, and lose their lives to substance-related diseases.

Your mental health can be severely affected, too. For example, there is a long history of research linking heavy alcohol usage and anxiety. We have already mentioned marijuana and paranoia. A particularly disturbing side-effect of marijuana is psychosis, where someone sees, hears or feels things that are not there. I believe this is a lot more common than is generally known. People commonly hear voices that appear to be outside of their head or feel insects crawling on them that are not there. Or they might have delusions they firmly believe, often the idea that someone is out to get them. I have met clients who were totally convinced that the CIA or ISIS were after them and wouldn't use the internet for fear they would be tracked down; however, their fears were entirely delusional.

Marijuana-induced psychosis is well-documented, often affecting teenagers before their brains are fully mature, leaving them with long term problems. Alcohol-induced psychosis is also common among heavy drinkers. I remember one particular person, who had been sober for years, relating to me the story of how in his drinking days he would sit up at night on his bed in fear, believing wasps were swarming around him, although there were none.

Compared to drugs, substances in foods might seem unimportant. But looked at from the perspective of what they do to our moods, they are underestimated. Any parents reading this who have brought up children sensitive to additives and colourings in food will know the dramatic effects these substances can have on our emotions and behaviour.

Research into how food affects our feelings and mental wellbeing is in its early days. However, indications are that what is good for your physical health is also good for your mental health. There already exists a vast body of scientific research showing that diets high in fresh whole foods, especially vegetables and fruits, are far healthier for our bodies and longevity than diets high in processed foods, sugar, salt and refined carbohydrates like white flour. While the research on nutrition and mental wellbeing is sketchier, it seems to be pointing in the same general direction. For example, just recently, a report from the Nutrition Network of the European College of Neuropsychopharmacology confirmed that a Mediterranean diet - which is rich in whole foods, fruit and vegetables - guards against anxiety and depression.

To me, this is no surprise. It's not just what the Meditteranean diet includes that's important, it's what it doesn't include: processed food. Food is big business. Getting it right makes companies fabulously rich. Manufacturers of ready-to-eat food go to great lengths to ensure that their products include a mix of salt, sugars, fats and additives that give us that dopamine hit. In other words, they make foods that are addictive, and any form of addiction messes around with your brain and moods.

Look at comfort eating, for instance, where someone eats to alter their emotional state. Do comfort eaters consume fresh vegetables? No, of course not. A carrot might be good for you, but it won't change your mood. However, cookies and cakes will. So the comfort eater goes for processed foods. Such foods contain refined carbs which release quickly into your bloodstream leading to insulin spikes that send your mood up and down. You might feel better for a short while, as your taste buds get what they want and you get a dopamine hit, but the Law of Rebound applies to fast food as well as drugs, so your mood will drop soon after. You might end up worse than before. It's common for comfort eaters to have feelings of self-loathing after a binge, leaving them feeling lower than when they started.

Even though the science linking food and mental health is not yet conclusive, it makes common sense to adopt a healthier diet for your emotions, anyway.

- Firstly, if you switch to a healthy diet, you will have fewer worries about contracting major diseases. The biggest killers in western society – heart disease, diabetes, and obesity – are all linked to poor diet and processed foods. So having a healthy diet will give you peace of mind.

- Secondly, if you eat healthily, you will boost your immune system, resulting in fewer minor illnesses. This will help your moods because we naturally feel better in our heads when we feel well in our bodies.

- Thirdly, You won't get those insulin spikes that can dramatically affect your mood. Unrefined carbs, which you find in whole foods like wholewheat products, don't do that. They release much slower into your system than refined carbs, like white flour, keeping your mood more stable. So, the case for a diet of high in whole grains, fresh fruit and vegetables is persuasive for your emotional wellbeing.

So far in this chapter, we have looked at the effects of putting substances in your body to change your mood. But people also use behaviours, rather than substances, to alleviate emotional pain. This can be a good thing, and indeed this book encourages people to act to help themselves. But it depends on which behaviour. If you use gambling, unsafe sex, or risk-taking as a way of relieving stress, anxiety or low moods, you are potentially making things a whole lot worse.

Many behaviours seem innocuous at first. Social media, for example, can have its uses. I use it to keep in touch with other authors and we pass knowledge on to each other. In that way, it's beneficial. But as we discussed in the chapter on approval, it can easily lead to a compulsive need for praise, which can become a serious addiction. This erodes your self-esteem and opens up the route to anxiety and depression. It also robs you of focus. If I go on to Facebook to check my author group, I can find myself moments later dragged into some algorithmic rabbit hole that a skilful advertiser has led me down, and my focus is shot until I realize what has happened.

Many people spend hours every day locked into social media, compulsively checking their account through the day whenever they have a chance to take a sneaky look at their phone. I had social media business accounts myself which I set up to keep in touch with readers, but I have become so concerned about the way social media pokes its nose into your life and destroys your focus that I have switched to using my email group, where readers can talk to me in a private.

Swiping your phone is a compulsive behaviour that has become an epidemic. I'm writing this book on the coast of Portugal, a stunningly beautiful area. Yet on the beach and in the oceanfront cafes, you see people swiping away, oblivious to the jaw-dropping natural splendour right in front of them.

The combination of social media and smartphones is compelling and it hoovers up your time. If you get stressed because you feel that you never have time to do everything in your day, I suggest going on a social media detox. You will miss it at first, but then you will realize how much extra time you have in your day. You can get more done, or have more time for leisure. You will wonder how you ever had so much time to waste, watching all those videos of kittens on your phone.

Any behaviour taken to an extreme can cause potential addiction problems. In my book "Change Your Life Today", I recounted the story of a lady whose hoarding had become so out of control that she was burying possessions in the garden because her house was full. Yet she had started out just collecting a few knick-knacks and ornaments for her home. Any activity where you are doing something that you know is out of control, but you do it anyway, meets my definition of addiction. It's being in two minds again: the addictive behaviour is based in your emotional mind and although your logical mind keeps telling you it's wrong, your more powerful emotional brain wins the argument.

We have discussed in this book the role that excessive adrenaline plays in emotional imbalance. Yet I often see people deliberately stirring up situations against their better judgement. They know it's likely to end badly for them but cannot stop themselves. They cause arguments and fights that are unnecessary. It may be that they have developed a kind of dependence on the same adrenaline that provokes stress and anxiety in the first place. I have heard clients say they have become addicted to the chaos, and cannot stop themselves causing more, even though it hurts them. In these situations, rebound occurs again, this time in the form of guilt or self-loathing when the logical brain kicks in, and they later reflect on their behaviours, making them feel worse than they did before they started acting out.

Dopamine plays a key role in how we become dependent on these behaviours. To get through life, we need to develop certain mental programs that we can run repeatedly, our own internal software that we can turn on whenever we need them, namely habits. We learn habits through trial and error. When we get something right, our brain rewards us with a blast of dopamine. That feels good, so we repeat the behaviour and the habit forms. But as this habit-forming process is just as effective for creating bad habits as good ones, we end up with addictions to substances, behaviours, or both.

So, if addictive habits change our moods for the worse and mess about with our emotions, it would obviously be a good idea to change those habits. But how many times have you decided to change such behaviours? Probably many times. How many times have you succeeded? Probably not so often. Maybe never.

If you have one negative habit, then at least it's clear where you need to take action. But if you are a typical human being, you likely have many negative habits, some more obvious than others. Knowing where to start and what to prioritize to have the biggest impact makes dealing with these behaviours much easier.

In the next chapter, we will look at how.

The Habits Audit.

Most of my work over the last few years has been helping people deal with negative behaviours and the emotional fallout they cause. Clinical assessments throw up all sorts of issues. People don't come in through the front door with one neat issue that needs to be addressed that is isolated from everything else in life. They have multiple issues that interconnect.

Clients come to me because they don't know where to begin, so the start point has to be making some sense of chaos. If you can get some order in your thinking, it all becomes a whole lot easier.

This is a job for your logical mind. But when it comes to addictions and compulsive behaviours, your emotional brain will try to take over. It will try to convince you that these behaviours aren't a problem. The reason it does this is that your emotional brain associates change with danger, which sometimes is true. But it doesn't differentiate, so it persuades you to carry on doing what you always do, even if what you always do is toxic. This is why you meet people who are in total denial about the dangers of smoking or eating processed red meat, even though the scientific evidence is screaming out warnings. Their emotional minds have convinced them that there's no need to change.

The solution is to consciously use your logical mind to look at your behaviours under the spotlight of total honesty. If you don't like something you see, that's okay, because you have just identified where you can take action, eliminate the problem and free up space in your life for more satisfaction and happiness.

To help you do this easily, I suggest you do a habits audit. It will take just a few minutes, will organize your thoughts for you and give you a simple list of where you need to take action and where you can relax.

To begin, think back to the last day you had that was a normal, routine day in your life. Maybe you only need to go back to yesterday. Or if you are reading this late at night, you might want to use the day you are finishing right now. Find some paper and write down everything you can remember that you did that was habitual, so anything you would be likely to do on a normal day.

I want the list to be yours, but to help you, here are a few suggestions:

- The time you got up.
- Your morning routine.
- What you wore.
- What you ate.
- Where you went.
- Who you talked to.
- Work you did.
- Internet use.
- Jobs you did at home.
- Watching TV.
- Playing games.
- Other recreation.
- Going out in the evening.
- Medication or other drugs you took.
- Who you socialized with.
- When you went to bed.

You can probably add a lot more ideas. Remember, it's routine habits we're looking for.

When you have your list, I want you to go through them and categorize them as:

- Good for me.
- Bad for me.
- Neither good nor bad.

I leave it up to you to decide what is good and bad for you, as I want to avoid putting my values on your life. But remember to be totally honest. This is where you need to consciously use your logical mind. For instance, if your emotional mind tells you that smoking 40 cigarettes and drinking a litre of vodka every day is good for you because you feel less stressed, well, how does that stand up under the spotlight of total honesty? Probably not that good.

Now use the Scale of Ten system. Go through the "goods" and give each one a score for how good you think it is for you. Then go through the "bads" and score each one for how bad it is for you. You can forget about the "neithers" – I don't want you wasting your time thinking about changing things that are neutral – that's just the day-to-day stuff we need not concern ourselves with.

Look at your top-scoring "good". Ask yourself, is there a way I can do more of this? Would that help me? So if your highest scoring "good" was that you get some exercise, would doing more help? If you're already in training for a triathlon, probably not, so look at the next highest scoring item on your list. But if by exercise you mean walking to your car, then you have found an area doing more can make a difference and make a plan to change for the better.

Then look at your top-scoring "bad". Is there a way to do less of that or stop? If you find that you constantly sabotage yourself, that might be the top of your "bads" and something you want to stop. If you know you eat too much, you cannot stop completely, but you can construct a plan to help you reduce your consumption.

Using a habits audit, you can quickly see where you can make the biggest impact on your wellbeing. However, you might be wondering how you go about it. No problem, I have your back. On Day Nine, I will introduce you to a proven way to make the most of your good habits and eliminate the bad ones. In doing this, you will solve many issues that cause you anxiety and lead you to emotional balance.

So keep your habits audit for Day Nine. You will need it then. But first, tomorrow, we need to sort out two nasties that have been causing you pain, so they don't derail you in future: negativity and procrastination.

Day Eight.

Negativity.

Negativity takes root when someone's expectations are repeatedly unfulfilled. This could be because of misfortune or, more frequently, unrealistic expectations. But whichever is the case, over time, a disillusion with life sets in.

When you feel you are not achieving in life, or not measuring up to your own or other people's expectations, that challenges the ego. It makes you feel uncomfortable, as you don't want to admit you are at fault, so you complain that the world is against you, or that you are unlucky, or that you just need a break, or whatever soundbite works best when you are explaining your lack of achievement to anyone who wants to listen. It's easier to blame external forces for your lamentable state than admit it could be the result of your own actions or inaction.

To help shield you from any unpalatable suggestion that your view that the world is against you might be wrong, your emotional brain screens out evidence to the contrary, dismissing it as a blip. Meanwhile, evidence that agrees with your view is let through and used to build your belief that life is against you.

To achieve emotional balance, you need to root out negativity, or it will drag on your feelings forever. But a negative mindset that has built up over many years won't crumble quickly. Negativity becomes a deeply entrenched habit, a default way of reacting to what goes on in your world. In a perverse way, negativity can become comforting because it's what you're used to, your discomfort ironically becomes your comfort zone.

It's like your emotional mind acts as a gatekeeper. Then, if some bad news comes along, the emotional mind thinks "Hey, great! Bad news validates the world-view that life is a place of gloom. Come in, bad news, you are welcome." But if some good news comes along, the emotional mind says "Hey, good news, get out of here. You don't fit in with the negative world-view. You are an exception and we don't allow exceptions in."

So, for instance, let's say you hate your job. You think every day is awful. Then, on one occasion, you have a good day. To your surprise, you enjoy your work that day. Are you happy? No, not if you suffer from negativity, because your emotional brain will tell you that it was just an exception and exceptions need to be ignored. Tomorrow you will be back to the usual drudgery.

Many people go through their whole lives thinking like this. No wonder there are so many unhappy people. But you don't have to be like that if you can provide one magic attribute: willingness to change. I am betting that if you have a negative mindset, you would like to change, you just don't know how to. But I believe in you because I have evidence that you want something different, that you are sick and tired of feeling sick and tired. How do I know this? Because you have bought this book.

I have good news for anyone bringing willingness to the problem of negativity. You can overcome years of negativity quickly if you put into action a few important concepts. It's time to change your default from negative to positive.

You might think that because I have used the word 'positive' that I'm going to start advocating positive thinking, but I am not. Positive thinking has a lot going for it. I would rather be a positive thinker than a negative one. But I believe positive thinking has a couple of flaws. If you have ever tried positive thinking, it didn't work, did it? The problem is that positive thinking becomes exhausting. It's like willpower – it works for a while, but ultimately you fall back into your negative default. I think the reason it's exhausting is that if you put a positive shine on everything, that includes the trash in your life. Who needs shiny trash? You need to get rid of it.

A much better concept is Solution-Focused Therapy (SFT). If you have read my other books, you will know I'm keen on SFT, and with good reason. It works, and it works quickly. I use it all the time. And regarding overcoming negativity, it's perfect, because SFT reprograms your emotional brain to think in the opposite.

Let me explain. You will remember that the negative mental gatekeeper rejects the exception. It argues that because it is the exception, you can ignore it. Exceptions, it believes, are unimportant.

However, a solution-based positive gatekeeper would work in the opposite way. It looks for exceptions and welcomes them in. Why? Because the exceptions are the clues to finding a better and happier life.

Let's go back to that example of the unexpected good day in a job you hate. The negative gatekeeper wants to reject that because it was the exception. But if you are using solution-focused thinking, you would seize on that exception. You would want to investigate that day to find out what made it better. Then, when you worked out what went right that day, you would look to see if you could repeat the good stuff. Makes sense, doesn't it?

Here's an example of how I'm using SFT in my work right now. A few years ago, I ran a 10-day course. It worked well for those who attended. So, using an SFT approach, I considered how I could use the format again. I ran more courses. They worked, too. So using SFT, I looked at how I could use the format to reach more people and came up with the idea of using it in a book. I did. Now I'm getting emails every day from readers telling me how it changed their lives. So then I looked at how I could apply SFT again to the subject of emotions, and you are now holding the result, this book.

With negative thinking, you go looking for the negatives and ignore positive exceptions. With SFT, you seize on the positive exceptions. If you keep repeating this way of thinking, it will become your new default. As for the negatives, there's no point in shining the trash, it's time to throw out what doesn't work for you.

We can sum SFT up in one sentence: do more of what works and stop doing what hurts. It seems so obvious when you look at it that way, but most people seem to do the reverse.

Let's look at a way you can use it today. Think about the relationships you have with people – not just close relationships, include work colleagues and acquaintances. Note down their names.

Do you remember in the habits audit how you labelled the "goods" and the "bads"? We can now use this simple system for negativity.

Looking at your list of names, which of them would you say had a negative outlook? Put an "N" by their names. Are many of the people in your world negative? Possibly they are. Negative people stick together because it feels good to complain about the world with someone who will reinforce your gloomy outlook, rather than talk with a positive person who might make you feel uncomfortable. Now put a "P" next to the people you would regard as being positive.

A good start to turning around your negativity would be to spend less time with the negative people (if you must see them at all) and more with the positive ones. That might make you feel uncomfortable, especially if the people you have labelled with an "N" are your best buddies, but do you really want to stay in the doldrums with them forever?

Now turn your attention to what's going on in your life currently. List the negative things that are going on. Are there things you can do less of? Are there things you can stop entirely? Then look at the positives. What's going on that's okay? Don't say nothing. There is always something – probably quite a few things if you look closely. The good things might not be good all of the time, and they might not be spectacular (yet) but remember we are looking at the building blocks, the things to get you going.

Are you involved in a project or job that is causing you stress or anxiety? You can apply SFT to this. Look at what you are doing, look for what's working, and then do more of that. Remember also to look at what's not working and see if you can do without that.

Look at what you have written. That should leave you with plenty of ideas for the start of an action plan. But how do you know where to start? You might know this by now - you use the Scale of Ten to prioritize. Then, how do you decide on your course of action? We will look at that tomorrow. For today I want you to develop the habit of looking for the exceptions in your life, the things that are good, and see if you can do more of them. Over time, this has an amazing cumulative effect. You find you are doing good stuff most of the time. It's hard to remain in a negative mindset when things are going your way.

Procrastination.

There is one stick-in-the-mud in your life that, even as you are reading this, could be trying to hold you back and undermine your break from negativity.

Procrastination, negativity's sidekick, is probably telling you it all sounds too much like hard work, or it will never work, or perhaps you could put off taking action until tomorrow, or maybe next week, or maybe sometime-never. Procrastination is good at firing out thought-bombs with alluring thoughts of just putting up your feet and doing nothing. Ahhh, doesn't that feel better? Well, no it doesn't, or you wouldn't be reading a book about emotional pain. Procrastination robs you of a better tomorrow by sabotaging today.

The negative mindset is inherently pessimistic. It sits like a judge, passing sentence on your future and finding it guilty of bringing more frustration and despondency. If that is what you're expecting, then it's not surprising you would procrastinate. Why make an effort if all that lies ahead is more gloom, frustration and disappointment? It becomes a self-fulfilling prophecy. You expect that the future will be rubbish, so you make no effort to help yourself, and when you reach that future point, guess what? That's right, it's rubbish.

But while the real culprit is procrastination, your emotional mind is soothing you with gentle lies, telling you that you're are hard-done-by, that you're unlucky, that you just need a break, that no one appreciates you, that the world is against you, and so on. In fact, it will tell you anything that will shield you from the truth, which is that the only person responsible for your happiness is you, not your family, not your friends, not your boss, not Santa Claus, it's you. Ouch, that hurts, so you don't think about it and procrastinate some more.

Occasionally, your logical brain might intervene and tell you that you need to get a grip, that putting things off has got to stop. You think about this and tell yourself you need to change. Perhaps you might buy a self-help book on procrastination. Do you have one on your bookshelf or e-reader already? You read about what to do. You decide that this is the big moment, you are going to get your life going. But it's such a huge effort, you become exhausted, and negativity and procrastination welcome you back to the fake comfort of inertia.

Your emotional mind tells you that this self-help business isn't all it's cracked up to be, it has let you down. It protects you from the truth that you are responsible for your own self-help, that it's not enough to read a book and understand its theory, you must apply its lessons in the real world. Knowledge without action is just chatter, but procrastination tells you that action is just too much effort. Procrastination never tells you not to do something, although that's its intention, instead, it dangles the idea that it might get done some time, which makes you feel better about doing nothing. It says things like:

- That can wait until tomorrow.
- You deserve a day off.
- That can wait until next week.
- You're tired, better sleep on it.
- That can wait until after the holiday.
- Hey, you can't do it today, it's Saturday.
- That can wait until after the election.
- You'd better wait until your horoscope improves.
- You need to read another self-help book first.
- Hey, let's buy pizza and watch TV instead!

Procrastination knows how to appeal to your weaknesses.

So how do you deal with it? Procrastination is a negative cycle. It goes like this: disappointment leads to procrastination which leads to lack of achievement which leads to disappointment in life which leads right back to procrastination, and so on and on endlessly.

You might be disillusioned with your career, for instance, and this makes you think that your work life will always be a disappointment, so instead of taking action to get a new career, you procrastinate because your emotional mind says "What's the point? It will just be a new disappointment." So you do nothing and things stay the same, which leads to more disillusion with work, and so the cycle goes on.

You might be in an uninspiring relationship, but because you are used to your relationships being unfulfilling, you procrastinate about improving it. This leads to more disillusion with your relationship, and you continue in the same sorry loop.

You can end up in a negative cycle like this forever. Many people do. Breaking out is easier said than done, especially if you try to use willpower. Because each of the three parts of the cycle reinforces the next ad infinitum, the procrastination loop is constantly strengthening. Every time you go through the cycle, the neural pathway in your brain becomes ever more entrenched. You can see the similarity to the power of an addictive behaviour, as we have already discussed. So if you try to break out with willpower, the strength of the cycle is likely to overpower your efforts, which will only reinforce it even more. If you are in such a cycle, it's not surprising if your life seems empty or unfulfilling.

If this all sounds pessimistic, however, don't worry. There is a solution to breaking out of the procrastination loop, and it isn't that difficult. You need to use your logical mind to help you establish a positive routine that will get you set you up to make progress in your life. This is a routine that will give you momentum, and then things start to happen. Momentum is a wonderful thing. It creates its own energy, which is why it doesn't exhaust you, instead it propels you along. Your job is just to carry out the action that will start the process.

What you're looking for is something that will start you off. Don't overthink this. Look at your morning routine. What do you do? Do you take forever to get going? Or do you set the alarm for the latest time possible, then drag on your clothes, throw a coffee down your throat and fall out of the door? Or if you're not working or retired, do you lie in bed, your mind going round in unproductive rumination?

Whatever your morning routine, is it one that demonstrates self-respect?

There's an old piece of advice that has stood the test of time: Get up. Dress up. Show up. If you apply that to your morning routine, you can make change happen quickly.

Starting with getting up, that means getting up rested and clear-headed at an hour that leaves you time to do whatever is necessary. This is the key action step that starts the chain of events going. This is the only bit of willpower you need to summon up because if you get this right, momentum will kick in and move you along.

My best advice is not to give yourself any thinking time between waking up and taking that first action. Not even a minute. If you do, your emotional mind will have time to convince you to procrastinate. So don't wait, count to five then go. Don't hit the snooze button, hit the shower instead. Your emotional mind will kick up a fuss, telling you to stop this crazy behaviour. The thought-bombs will be flying. But if you're already up and moving, you have momentum on your side and that's one thing that will overcome your emotional mind's objections.

Getting this first action in place is so important because everything flows from that. I wrote an article on this subject called *Don't Wait Until You're Ready*, and I have reproduced that in the resources section at the end of this book. If you think you will have difficulty in making that first morning move, please read it when you have finished this chapter.

Next, plan how you will dress up for the day. This is your self-respect move. It is a statement of intent. It shows the world how you want to be seen. Also, it tells your emotional brain how you want to be seen. When you look in the mirror, your emotional brain is watching. If you dress like you could not care less, your subconscious mind will absorb that message and will reflect it back to you all day long in negative thoughts about you and your life. But if you dress like you mean it, your subconscious will support your intent. What you wear should be appropriate for the day's activities. You wouldn't wear a sharp business suit to take your kids out to the park. It's about looking like you respect yourself, whatever you are wearing.

Not only will the way you dress create an impression on your own subconscious, but it will also send out a subliminal message to the people you meet, from strangers to your close family. If you look as though you care about yourself, you can expect others to treat you more respectfully than if you look like something the dog has dragged out of a hedge.

Finally, think about turning up for your day in an engaged way, not just going through the motions. Whether you're going to the office, taking the kids to school, attending appointments, or just staying home, engage with it. This is your life. If it isn't what you want, okay, we will look at what to do about that in the next chapter. But for today, this is what you have, so take part in it. People who spend their lives worrying about the future or regretting the past are missing out on their lives. They feel like they are a spectator on a life that's passing them by. If you still struggle with taking part in your life in the present, try going back to the Active Awareness chapter and running through that again.

So today, I want you to plan your routine for tomorrow. I want you to plan how you will get up, dress up and turn up to your life tomorrow.

Then when you have done that, you will be ready tomorrow to move on to the really exciting stuff: how you can eliminate the problems that cause you stress and anxiety.

Day Nine.

Action.

Today I am going to share with you a strategy that will completely transform your problems and lead to much greater happiness and contentment in your life. That's a big promise, but I know I can deliver. What you will read next has been thoroughly tested in the real world. I have used this strategy successfully with numerous clients in my practice.

This works.

What's more, it works for most things that you want to achieve in life or ridding you of the negatives that weigh on you emotionally.

Intrigued? Let's jump in.

To begin, I want you to consider again for a moment what we were discussing about the futility of worrying about the future and obsessing about past events. All that you achieve is higher levels of stress and anxiety. Additionally, the frustration you feel at not being able to solve your issues will cause you to become more negative. You might feel that life is unfair, that you can't manage, that hope is draining away.

You might have even given up already and find that you can't muster the motivation to try anymore. You have become frozen into inaction. You might have seen that the title of this chapter is *Action* and thought you cannot do that. Or conversely, perhaps you run yourself into the ground, frantically trying everything you can think of to resolve issues, but without success. You might feel you take too much action already. Many people go through their lives in this unsatisfactory state. But you don't have to be one of them. The solution is in this chapter, a very specific plan of action.

To make progress, you firstly need to understand what you want. Most people do not. If you had a physical illness, explaining what would make you feel better would be simple - you will be better when the illness has gone. But when we mean feeling better emotionally, it can all become somewhat vague. How exactly will you know when you feel better? If you feel better tomorrow than you feel today, will that be enough?

When I ask clients what they want, some will say something like, "I just want to feel happy." This sounds reasonable enough on the surface, but when you look closely, it's impossible to define, as it's a moving target. This is because we all live in a range of emotions every day. If you think about it, you must have low points to appreciate the high points, so you cannot feel happy without experiencing the opposite sometimes. Much of the time, we are in an average state. It's necessary to accept that you will always be in an emotional range and that you will never be on the upside all the time. But what you can do is move your range up, so that the average state you are in most of the time is much more acceptable to you. This means that your lows will be more tolerable and your highs will feel higher. That all makes sense, but that still leaves the question of how we quantify what we want – in other words, how will you recognize that you have found what you want when you get there, and how to achieve it. You will need to sort those things out in that order. It's impossible to achieve what you cannot explain in the first place.

If your mind is scattered, you will make little headway. You might even go backwards. The solution is to find some focus. Do you remember in the Habits Audit, I asked you to do an exercise that would give you a list of things that would make the biggest improvement in your life? I want you to expand on this now. To do this, I want you to write down the issues that concern you about your future. What exactly are they? There might be just one major issue that is worrying you. But more likely there will be many. Make the list as long as you like. You might find that getting everything down on paper helps stop your mind churning.

Look through your list and cross out any that are impossible to resolve. For instance, if you worry about whether there is an afterlife, you cannot solve that one. Focusing on a question that you cannot answer, except by faith, is likely to increase your anxiety. But if you worry about money, passing an exam, relationships, housing, career, your weight, or anything that is resolvable, leave those on the list.

Go through the items on your list and scale them, giving each item a score out of ten for how important each one is to you. Which issue, if you could resolve it, would make the biggest positive impact on your life? It may be that you have one issue dominating your life at present that is dragging you down, in which case it will be clear where you should be concentrating. But it's best to break down large issues. Look at what aspects of the problem you can deal with. What are they exactly? Which aspect is the priority?

If there is no one single dominant issue in your life, but instead you have a general dissatisfaction and a sense of low mood that you want to deal with, look at your environment.

What I mean by environment is your day-to-day world, such as your home, the area you live in, who you live with, your relationships, what you do for work, and how you spend your leisure time. Early in this book, we discussed how your emotional brain is constantly scanning the data it picks up from your senses and feeds it back to you in thoughts and feelings. If our emotional brain is reacting negatively to the information it receives, it will make you feel negative, therefore, addressing areas that are lacking in your environment will help you feel more contented.

So, go through your list, scale the items, and see what comes out as the top target for you to address. Draw a ring around the one with the highest score and underline it. You have found your focus, and resolving that issue gives you a goal. Having a goal is a wonderful thing. It reduces the scattering of your thoughts, increases your emotional health, and makes the future something to look forward to, rather than something to fear. You get immediate benefits because it gets your logical brain in the driving seat, which helps to quieten all the unhelpful background chatter from your emotional mind. Moreover, if you can eliminate, or at least lessen, the major issues that keep you awake at night, your life must improve and your average daily emotional state will get better. I don't mean it *might* get better, it *will* get better. No other outcome is possible.

But how are you going to reach that goal you have just created?

That's where the fun begins.

I first evolved the following strategy working with outpatients in therapy for self-sabotaging behaviours. I found my clients could apply it to a wide range of subjects. I've seen it work for things as diverse as solving a phobia to starting a business – that's versatile! I first wrote about this strategy in my book "Change Your Life Today" and had enthusiastic feedback from readers who tried it and found it did indeed change their lives. I use this strategy in my life all the time. It's the basis of every new project I take on, such as writing this book. It works for everyone who follows the simple rules, so it will work for you, too, if you apply it to your goal.

It's called The Path. You notice I spell Path with a capital letter. That's because it's not just any old path. The Path is a powerful concept that will make achieving the goal of resolving your key issue not just possible, but inevitable. When you have a Path, you cannot fail.

To begin, I want you to imagine that your goal is on a distant hill. You might imagine your goal looks like a bright, shining star. Or it could be the face of a happier you. Whatever works best for you. Between you and the goal, imagine there are hills and valleys, woods and rivers. You don't know how to get to the goal. You can see it, but you are frustrated because can't find a way to reach it. That's why this issue has been causing you anxiety.

But imagine that suddenly, as if by magic, a track appears at your feet and it runs all the way to your goal. This is your Path. Now getting to your goal becomes inevitable. All you have to do is to move forward and stay on your Path. If you do those two things, you will reach your goal. No other outcome is possible.

Path is an acronym. It stands for: *planning and total honesty*. Let's look at planning first.

You need a plan. This should be something that has been tested. Thinking about the issue you want to resolve, what has worked for other people? Can you copy someone else's methods? Does a course exist to solve your issue? Is there an off-the-shelf solution you can use? Are there apps or web sites dedicated to what you want to achieve that can guide you? Is there an expert you can go and see who can advise you? Is there a treatment you can use? Is there a course you can enrol on? Getting the right plan for your Path is crucial.

People fail because they don't have a plan or have a poor one. But using a plan that others have used successfully will give you a solid basis for your Path. So don't try to be a genius – use a plan that others have had success with. Be selective and make sure that the plan you choose has a credible track record.

Once you have selected a plan, you then need to decide on your daily step. This is at the heart of the Path strategy. Your daily step is the minimum action that you need to do to keep you moving along your Path. It should be something that you know you can achieve. It should stretch you a little bit, but not so much that you give up because it's too hard. You need to commit to it. Your daily step should be the biggest priority of your day. It's a no-fail action.

You don't necessarily need to do it every single day. That depends on your plan. For instance, imagine you want to get fit. You go and see a professional to design you a plan. He advises you that, as you haven't stepped inside a gym for twenty years, you would probably fail if your target was to work out every day. But if you commit to three times a week, you are being realistic. So you would use your daily plan three times weekly.

Here's another example. Let's say you want to do a meditation course to help prevent low moods. If you've never done it before and tried meditating for an hour every day, that would probably be too much, and you would give up after a few days. But if you committed to a daily plan of doing 15 minutes, 5 days a week, that would be comfortably achievable. Research has shown that someone who does that will reduce their chances of a recurrence of depression after just a month of following a meditation program like that. So just doing your daily step of 15 minutes per day, 5 times per week, would take you along the Path to your goal. You just need to focus on those daily steps, and getting to your goal becomes inevitable.

Then we come to total honesty. Why is that part of the Path? Well, if for any reason you don't do your daily step, you need to be totally honest with yourself about the reason. If, for instance, you have committed to getting counselling twice a week to overcome an issue and one time you don't go, be honest with yourself about why that is. If you had the flu, that's a good reason. If you didn't go because you felt tired, however, ask yourself in all honesty, was that a good enough reason, or were you procrastinating? Not taking your daily step is like leaving your Path.

The only way your Path can fail is if you don't take your daily step. If you keep taking the steps along your Path, success is the only possible outcome.

You can have more than one Path, especially if they are complimentary. My current goal is to write this book. My daily step is to write one thousand words minimum, five days a week. I don't waste my mental energy worrying about if I can do it or when I will finish it because I know that if I keep taking my daily step, my success is assured. But I also know that writing is sedentary, which isn't healthy, so I have another daily step of walking at least four miles every day to keep me fit. These are my non-negotiable commitments currently.

Using a Path to resolve a major worry is massive. Instead of pointless ruminating, you get rid of the issue altogether. The simple discipline of taking a daily step that you know you can achieve makes overcoming most things in life possible. It drags you out of negativity.

What's more, by giving you focus and concentrating your attention on the daily step, away from worry about the future and regret about the past, it keeps you in the day, and that's where you find contentment and greater happiness.

Hypnotherapy.

In this book, we have discussed how we can compare the subconscious, emotional mind to a computer, and how we can reprogram it to run the software (our thoughts and feelings) that we want. Hypnotherapy does exactly that. It explains to the emotional brain the changes in your thoughts and feelings that you want.

In my early days working as a therapist, I was sceptical of hypnotherapy. I had confused it with stage hypnosis, as you see on TV, which is a trick. But I had a problem. No matter what I tried, I could not give up smoking. I had fought and lost with nicotine addiction for years. You name it, I had tried it. In desperation, I tried hypnotherapy, as it seemed to have a successful track record with smoking.

I have written about giving up smoking in other books. But previously I have not revealed the role hypnotherapy played in my quitting. This was because I was concerned that readers might focus solely on hypnotherapy, think it was a magic bullet and that all they needed to do was to pay a hypnotherapist for a one-off session and it would cure their problems. It isn't like that.

What happened with my smoking taught me a lot about hypnotherapy. I learned that it was not a one-time use therapy. You need to use it regularly. I had naively expected that one session would cure me of cravings for nicotine. I was disappointed. After my first session, I wanted to smoke right away. But I had been told I needed to use it for a while, so I kept listening to recordings while relaxing.

I realized that I was becoming more receptive. At first, I had found it hard to relax, I felt unsettled and was waiting for the recording to end. But after a few attempts, I found I was drifting off into a profound state of relaxation. When the recording brought me back up at the end, I had the sensation of surfacing from a place deep inside of me. I could hardly remember what had happened or what had been said on the recording, but I felt that in those sessions, something was working. It seemed that in the sessions where I listened to every word and failed to drift off, I made less progress. This carried on for a couple of few weeks. I listened to the recordings several times. I was enjoying the relaxation of the deeper sessions, but I was still smoking.

Then it happened. Out of the blue one evening, I suddenly quit. I hadn't planned to quit at that moment. It took me by surprise. It wasn't easy. I endured massive cravings for weeks, and I still had to use motivational tools such as those I write about in my books.

But there was one thing that made this attempt different from all my previous failed attempts: *I had no doubt that I would succeed.* It wasn't determination, it was more like an invisible force was keeping me from smoking. I put that down to the hypnotherapy because nothing else was different. It was the only new factor. That was in 2012. I never smoked again. Since then, I have experimented more with hypnotherapy and feel that it is a valid treatment to use as part of a wider therapeutic package. I think it can be particularly helpful with emotional issues, especially anxiety.

Antonia Ryan, who is a hypnotherapist working with me, first used hypnotherapy herself as a customer when she could not pass her driving test. She knew all the theory and could drive competently, but in the test's atmosphere, her nerves would get the better of her. So she consulted a hypnotherapist and passed at the next attempt.

With this book, I have included a hypnotherapy download, written and narrated by Antonia. If you haven't already downloaded this with the other audios, go to https://www.subscribepage.com/emotions_audio. When you have logged in, you will see a link to the MP3 audio downloads page. You will also get an email from me that gives you a link to the audios. (If you cannot get your audios with either of the above methods, send me an email to emotions.downloads@gmail.com and an autoresponder will email you back with an alternative link immediately.)

I left hypnotherapy to near the end of the book for three reasons. Firstly, I felt it important that you learned the cognitive tools first. Secondly, you have already had the mindfulness and relaxation downloads to listen to for a few days. Thirdly, hypnotherapy is part of the aftercare program to follow on from the 10-day course.

Hypnotherapy works in a complementary but quite different way to mindfulness. The mindful therapy you have been listening to trains your logical mind to analyse the output of your emotional mind. It shows you that thoughts and feelings are not facts and that they are not instructions you have to obey, either.

Hypnotherapy, on the other hand, bypasses your logical mind and talks directly to your emotional brain. Whereas in mindfulness, you are trained to bring your attention back to the present if your conscious thoughts drift off, with hypnotherapy it doesn't matter, because the recording continues to speak directly to your subconscious even though your logical brain has gone off in a different direction. In fact, it's no problem even if you fall asleep during hypnotherapy because your subconscious never sleeps and will continue listening to the recording.

To prepare yourself for your first hypnotherapy session, you will need to find half an hour when you won't be disturbed. You need to be comfortable and warm. If you are giving your senses comforting information to feed through to your emotional brain, it will be more receptive to the hypnotherapy.

You are best listening to the recording on a headset to help shut out the outside world. Make yourself really comfortable. I suggest lying down on a bed or couch. Put a blanket over yourself if that helps you feel more at ease and warm. Now all you have to do is listen.

All being well, the recording will take you down into a deeply relaxed state where your logical mind will be quiet and your emotional mind will be receptive and focused on the recording. This state is sometimes called trance. Personally, I don't like that word, as it suggests to some people you have lost control. But you have not. It's a state we can get into when we are focused on anything, even watching TV. So don't worry, if you need to rouse yourself quickly, you can. If you go into a deep state, the recording will bring you back to the present moment at the end.

You might find that the first time you try this, it's quite blissful, as you get into deep relaxation. But equally, you might find that it's hard to settle the first time and you cannot seem to get into it. That's hardly surprising if you are used to having stress or anxiety in your life and your default setting is running on adrenaline. If you cannot settle, you might find using the Dynamic De-stress exercise before you start the hypnotherapy helps you wind down and gets you in a better frame of mind. You might find, like me, that you need a few attempts before you become more receptive.

Some people naturally take to hypnotherapy quicker than others. For a few, it doesn't work. It is crucial that you go into using it with an open mind. If you think to yourself that this is just some old mumbo-jumbo that will never work, then it won't because your emotional brain will sabotage you every time. That's the thing with hypnotherapy. You need to want it to work. If you don't believe it has a chance, I guarantee it won't work for you. Your disbelief will become a self-fulfilling outcome. But you have nothing to lose by trying. At worst, it should help you relax more, which is no bad thing.

Day Ten.

The Process.

Congratulations!

You have covered so much over the last 9 days. As we arrive at Day 10 of your program, I want to give you a default process to work with, so on days when the going gets difficult, you have a plan to fall back on.

This has been a rich course. You only have to look back on the chapter titles to confirm this. I could have written one book on procrastination, then another on anger, and so on, but I wanted to write one good book that covered many related needs, a book that could transform lives quickly, and I had faith in you that you could absorb all this.

If you have stuck to the course as I wrote it, and carried out my daily suggestions, you will have taken on an ambitious program of concepts. Your mind, on both a logical and emotional level, will be digesting it all for some time to come. Even if you have only followed up 50% of my suggestions, you will have tackled more self-improvement concepts in 10 days than many people cover in 10 years. Indeed, if you have taken to heart and absorbed the content of just one single chapter, you will have new knowledge that will improve your life forever.

On a good day, when you are untroubled, the information in these chapters is accessible and straightforward to apply to your life, especially after you have practised them for a while. But on a bad day, when you need it most and your thinking is fragmented, you need a process to hold on to. This is it. The process falls into three parts:

- Assessment.
- Decision.
- Engagement.

Assessment.

When your mood changes, the first step is to assess what is going on. In the past, when your emotional brain ran your life all the time, you would not have done this, you would have acted on what your emotional brain told you to do. But this book has shown you how to step back and look at your incoming thoughts and feelings, rather than react immediately.

The trigger event for your change of mood might be obvious: someone might suddenly say something upsetting, you might receive bad news, or you might feel physical pain. Putting in that pause before action to assess what's going on can save you much emotional pain later. This is because your emotional brain reacts faster than your logical mind, therefore your first reaction will be emotional, not rational.

Consequently, your first idea is unlikely to be your best. Remember, a sudden drop in mood is likely to trigger a thought-bomb, and they are always bad news. Give your logical brain a chance to catch up and see if your second idea is better. Ask yourself, on a scale of one to ten, how helpful would it be if I react in this way? If it's a low number, it's a bad idea.

Sometimes changes in mood can take time and be subtle, without an obvious trigger. In this instance, remember how your emotional brain is constantly monitoring your senses. Do you have a basic need that isn't being met? Are you lonely or bored? Do you need to eat or rest? Is your environment uninspiring and you need a change? Have you been in the company of negative people who have gradually dragged your mood down?

Occasionally, you might be unable to identify what has caused your mood to change. This happens. Our body chemistry is in constant flux. Hormonal changes beyond your control might be happening. You may never know.

Decision.

Having taken a moment to assess what has caused your mood change, your next step is to make a decision. Your choices are:

- Action.
- Letting go.
- Acceptance.

If you see that there is an action you can take to deal with the cause of your emotional downturn, scale it first, and if it comes out with a good score, do it. The key here is to get on with it quickly. If you have been suffering from negativity, a delay will cause procrastination, which will then lead to you ruminating about your difficulty, dragging your mood down even more.

So take action as soon as you have decided. The chapters on negativity and procrastination will help you, as will the essay Don't Wait Until You're Ready, which I've included in the bonus content of this book.

Maybe your action is just one thing that will put your day back on track, for instance, calling a friend when you're feeling lonely, or getting out in the countryside when you're feeling uninspired, or listening to one of the recordings when you're feeling anxious. Or maybe you need a longer-term strategy, such as a career change, in which case you can employ the Path concept. Either way, the sooner you start the better because when you take action, you will feel positive emotions like hope and optimism, and that will make your emotional brain turn up those nice neurotransmitters like serotonin, so you will feel better right away.

Even if your action doesn't achieve what you want, the positive emotions you get from taking action will carry you out of your low point, anyway. So next time you are thought-bombed by ideas like "I cannot be bothered" and "What's the point?" remember action makes you feel good; procrastination leads to misery. Feeling good or misery? That should be an easy choice.

Sometimes, the appropriate action is to let go of something. This can be a tough decision. You might need to let go of a long-cherished dream that you realize will never happen. You might need to let go of a person who has been important in your life. These are sad moments. But remember, we said very early in this book that sadness is not a negative feeling; it is the first step to recovering and feeling well again.

Letting go might take the form of releasing your desire to control. As we have discussed, trying to micromanage your life is a major cause of stress, and is ultimately futile, since situations are constantly changing and it's impossible to be on top of everything. Yet people cause themselves so much emotional pain trying to do so. At best, you might influence people or events in favour of your preferred outcome.

Readers who have older children will have experienced this. When our children are small, we are controlling with good reason, as the small person cannot adequately look after themselves. But as our children grow and perhaps develop ideas or ambitions we don't agree with, we want to interfere, leading to resentments and a deterioration in the relationship we cherish. Letting go of the parental instinct to control can be hard, but necessary, and ultimately beneficial to both.

In a work situation, the manager who tries to micromanage the personnel often has short-term success but runs into problems of staff retention and deteriorating morale because of resentment among the workers.

The urge to control comes from the belief that you are right. But although you might be convinced, it's just your opinion, and it's worth considering sometimes if what you want or believe is actually what is good for you or those around you. We can be blindsided to what is best for us because we cannot see what is really the best outcome. Often, this is because we cannot always know the possibilities available. For instance, you might be tenaciously holding on to a job that causes you emotional pain because you are afraid of losing your income. When you are laid off and forced to let go, you feel your world has ended. But the situation forces you to look at new options and you discover a much more suitable career that improves your income and happiness.

Letting go can also be unquestionably positive. It's a relief to let go of addictions, self-destructive behaviours, negative friends, resentments, anger, guilt, remorse and other draining emotions. Letting go can be like throwing out the clutter in your head. You might find, for example, that other people's goals for you have caused you unnecessary emotional suffering. It's often the case that we go through life trying to live up to the values of other people, like our parents, or what we consider to be society's norms. But living by other people's values brings angst and lack of fulfilment. If you spend years in law school because your parents want you to become a lawyer, when really you wanted to become a tennis pro, then getting your qualification to practice will leave you feeling empty inside. You have lived out another person's dream. It's good to kick out all the old attitudes that don't serve you any more, throw open the windows and let the light flood into your thinking.

Whereas action involves doing something, letting go is more about ceasing to do or believe something. By contrast, acceptance suggests leaving something as it is. This may seem rather lame, but it is not.

Acceptance might be a realization that something in your present reality is absolutely fine. We live in a culture that encourages us to go after the next shiny new thing, often leading us to overlook what is good already. Acceptance can bring an appreciation of what you have right now.

Acceptance is often the first step before taking action, letting go, or both. For instance, acceptance might mean coming to terms with a limiting factor in your life that you cannot change, so you can focus on what you can realistically achieve. Nowadays, we are bombarded by slogans and memes that implore us never to give up. There's a lot to be said for persistence in life, it can take you a long way, but if you are persisting in the pursuit of something unattainable, you are bringing frustration and other negative emotions into your life. Acceptance of this will not only stop the pain, but also open you up to what you can achieve and bring you pleasure.

Engagement.

Finally, having assessed what's going on for you, then decided whether to take action, let go or accept, your final stage is to engage.

Engagement means being fully involved in your changed behaviour. If you feel you are going through the motions, your mind will still be liable to ruminating on the future or reliving past pain. Engaging in what you are doing right now eliminates all that. It will take practice. Using Active Awareness is a good exercise to reinforce engagement.

Engagement is also highly productive. Therefore, in the concept of the Path, taking daily action is so crucial. If you commit to your daily action, you keep in the present moment and get things done. I am doing this myself right now, as I take my daily action of writing at least 1,000 words per day. I am nearing the end of this Path as this book is almost complete. But for you, this book is the beginning, so let's look at where you go from here in the next chapter.

After Day 10.

I want you to feel supported after you finish reading, so let's look ahead. You will need to practice what you have read, otherwise, your new skills will quickly go rusty and your old behaviours and ways of thinking will take over, just as a lovely garden will go to pot if no one maintains it. You might find it useful to go over the 10 days again, or you might prefer to focus on the parts of the book that have resonated with you most. I leave it up to you. But you shouldn't go far wrong if you bear in mind my philosophy of doing more of what works and leaving what doesn't.

Keep listening to the audios as much as you want and for as long as you want. If you have found the mindfulness useful, you will be interested to know that we are preparing a mindfulness book to compliment this book. It's called "Mindfulness for Stress and Anxiety" and is written by Antonia Ryan, who narrated the audios with this book.

I can also announce that "Emotions" will have a sequel: "Confidence". In that book, I will be developing the concepts you have become familiar with in "Emotions" and going into depth on such subjects as self-confidence, social anxiety and self-esteem. You can find out more about these books and check for release dates on our website WinsPress.com, where you will also find information on all our books and free-to-read content.

At the end of this book, there is a resources section. This is extra information for you to dip into. I intend to expand the resources section over time. In the past, when a book was published, that was the end of it. Nowadays, we have the flexibility of digital publishing, meaning that books can be changed and updated regularly. But you won't have to get a new edition of "Emotions" when an update comes out, as existing owners of this book will receive new content by email.

So, over the next few months, you can expect to receive occasional new articles and MP3s. You don't need to do anything to receive these, as your email address was added to the system when you opened an account for downloads. There is an unsubscribe link on every email, should you feel you have moved on and don't require my support anymore.

It is my profound hope that this book has helped you and will act as a springboard for a happier, more fulfilled life. If having read this book you feel you have deeper issues, I would urge you to consult your physician.

If you want to give me feedback on this book, just reply to one of my emails, and that will come directly to me. I'm always delighted to hear how my readers are getting on.

Finally, I would like to thank you for joining me on the journey through this book. I wish you joy and peace of mind.

Lewis David,

Portugal, February 2020.

Extra Resources

Emotional Attachment.

I am including below a chapter on emotional attachment from Antonia Ryan's forthcoming book, "Mindfulness for Stress, Anxiety and Negative Emotions" which will be available from WinsPress.com. We intend her book to be a complementary work for readers of "Emotions" who want to continue to learn more about Mindfulness.

In this chapter, we will look at what we mean by the term attachment and how our attachments can be at the root of anxiety, fear, and negative emotions. We see that attachment is a necessary and natural part of being human. We will discuss when and how attachments can become troublesome. We will discuss how an awareness of our own attachments can help us to become more conscious of our values, motivations, and assumptions about life. We will also look at the role attachments play in generating anxious thoughts and reactions.

In its more exaggerated form, attachment is a compulsive habit or addiction. As humans, we are hard-wired to attach to places, people, and things. This is part of our survival mechanism. As babies, we need to attach to our care-givers to ensure we have all the essentials to survive and prosper. If young children do not have a consistent, loving care-giver in their early days and years they suffer from 'attachment disorder' which can have huge implications for their later life. As we mature we need to make friends, form bonds with colleagues, neighbours, and so on. These attachments are all necessary for our emotional and mental health. Researchers such as Buettner have shown such bonds and support to help elongate a healthy life (see 'Blue Zones') and releases feel-good hormones such as serotonin. Since the dawn of time, humans have needed to be together to ensure safety and survival.

However, attachments can become tricky for us if we hang on to them too tightly. Things change, time moves on, people grow and develop. We need room in our lives to let our attachments change, grow and develop too as our lives move forward.

As our brains love familiarity we attach to places. You have had the experience of going away for a few days or weeks and on your return home have a rush of familiarity and a sense of 'coming home'. Perhaps you have moved cities or countries. I have and when I go 'home' to the country where I grew up I always have a rush of pleasure at being on 'home ground'. It's familiar and comfortable. I have an attachment to this place.

Do you have a favourite pair of shoes, pyjamas or slippers? They are cosy, comfortable and familiar. You are upset if you discover they have got mangled in the wash or are beyond repair.

Attachment is our brain's way of making sure we don't do anything too rash. Stick to the familiar and the safe options. By doing what is familiar, we feel safe. Having our object of attachment removed or rearranged in some way can generate feelings of anxiety. But see it for what it is: just an attachment to the familiar and known. By accepting this we can overcome feelings of alarm or anxiety.

Have you ever been in a group situation in which people had to find a seat themselves, perhaps a training course that meets for a few consecutive sessions, or a meeting that meets weekly or monthly? Have you noticed how people gravitate towards the same seats on each occasion? Or perhaps in a work situation in which you have a staff room, people have 'their' seat. As a newcomer, it can be very disconcerting to be told you need to move as you are sitting in 'Miss Black's chair'. People love being attached to things. These things are often things that are not even theirs to begin with.

You see this with children. The children are playing with toys in a playgroup or school and a child decides a toy belongs to them just because they play with it regularly. They are unwilling to share the toy. The child gets upset when someone else is playing with 'their' toy.

Perhaps you have been on holiday to a beautiful place out of season. It is quiet and you have the luxury of walking on empty beaches and always being able to get 'your' seat at your favourite restaurant. The grounds around the hotel are quiet and you can always get 'your' sunbed by the pool. However, you go back in July and you feel quite put out by all the crowds. You feel mildly upset that the friendly waiter at your favourite restaurant hasn't kept 'your' table by the window for you; actually, he hardly seems to remember you. You can't find any free sunbeds and the beach is so crammed by sunbathers you have to pick through them on your walk. It's all very disconcerting. You feel perhaps that the holiday has been spoiled as this place is not as you remembered it.

We can also be very strongly attached to our ideas and opinions. A casual scroll through Facebook shows just how attached to their opinions some people are. Just take a moment to consider this. Now, reflect on a recent debate or argument you have had. How fiercely did you defend your corner? How firmly did you hang on to your side of the argument? We will come back to this later. Remember to reflect on these aspects of behaviour with a spirit of curiosity and compassion.

Think about the strength or intensity of your reactions and ask why. What could this indicate about what is going on for you? For example, I remember once some years ago we had a family get together. My then ten-year-old son was present. He was talking excitedly about television adverts to his uncle. His uncle commented on how much television my son must watch in a joking sort of way. I immediately felt a rush of anger and upset. How dare he say my son watches too much television, of course he doesn't! Is he trying to insinuate I am a neglectful mother, and on and on. I think you probably get the picture. I said nothing. I appeared to ignore the comment and the conversation turned to something else.

However, when I took a few minutes to calm down, I thought about my reaction with a sense of compassion and curiosity. Was there any truth in this? Why did I react (albeit internally) so defensively? I realized that I had been extremely busy in the time leading up to this Christmas family gathering. I worked fulltime in a demanding job and had a home to run and a family to take care of. Perhaps my son had been allowed to watch a lot of television as I bustled about cleaning, cooking and trying to keep on top of the demands of my job which often involved work at home. This led me to think about how I could perhaps get some help at home. Perhaps get a cleaner for a few hours a week. Maybe relax my standards a bit. I could make simpler meals. Get shopping delivered. I talked to my son about activities he might like to do outdoors. We planned a camping trip. He joined a football club. We went for more walks along the beach and in the countryside. We spent some time on craft projects at home.

This reaction, which was painful and could have resulted in a big family bust-up, was actually a helpful wake-up call. I could have had a fight with my relative or chastised myself, heaping on the shame and guilt, I could have felt like a victim. Poor me, with all this work to do while he is just having a go at me. However, with a spirit of curiosity and compassion, the comment was the catalyst for a positive change to our routines. Looking back, I could thank my relative for this comment. The changes made meant that we made lots of happy memories doing lovely things that we would have missed out on if we had carried on mindlessly in the usual way.

In the above example, I was attached to the idea that I was a good mother, a conscientious employee and an effective housewife. How dare someone challenge this! I felt affronted and upset that my view of myself was being questioned. This experience cast light on my values. This is a good thing. By taking a curious approach to my feeling of discomfort triggered by an innocent comment, I could move closer to a better version of myself as a mother and to create some happy experiences for my son. I didn't get hung up on it; I just noticed it, made some adjustments and moved on.

The Pleasure Trap

In a book named The Pleasure Trap, Dr Doug Lisle explains in great detail how as humans we are programmed to seek pleasure and avoid pain. This makes sense when we consider our choices in food, home comforts and habits. It seems natural to enjoy foods that are satisfying and tasty. We like being warm and cosy, so we crank up the central heating. We avoid situations that make us feel physically or emotionally uncomfortable. We get attached to our comfortable habits and routines. This makes us feel safe and secure. Why not seek pleasure and avoid pain? It seems to be a natural and common sense thing to do. Why would anyone seek anything else? Who wants pain in their life?

Perhaps you fear any pain or discomfort – a natural response has become exaggerated. Any small threat you perceive to your comfort or security signals a red alert, triggering anxious thoughts. By seeing your disturbance as a natural, although not necessarily a rational response to a small infringement of your physical, emotional or mental comfort and attachment to pleasure, you can put your anxiety into perspective. It's an attachment to a certain state or feeling. Just because your boss looked at you with what you thought was a disapproving look doesn't mean you have to go into full-scale panic. It's an attachment to the good feelings of security and acceptance you get when your boss smiles at you. By being aware of our reactions we can start to get some control over the reactions we have when our attachments feel threatened in any way.

It is useful to consider your attachments for many reasons: it helps highlight areas of sensitivity in your life, perhaps you get a bit touchy if anyone criticizes your work. Why is this? Asking these sorts of questions can help uncover many aspects of your character and conditioning.

Attachments are a part of life and how we function as humans. Look on them as helpful barometers of our emotional health. The ferocity with which we hang on to an attachment can show where our values, expectations and assumptions about life are. By feeling the discomfort or pain around challenges to our attachments we can be more aware and present in our life. By practising this with compassion and gentleness you can uncover much about how you function.

We can do this Mindfulness practice of noticing attachments without harsh judgment or criticism. You might notice that you are very attached to an idea of yourself or another person which gets overturned by a reaction or response that seems uncharacteristic. Give yourself or the other person some leeway. Look on it as an opportunity to grow or let the other person grow. People do not always have to conform to our idea of who they should be. And we do not always have to fit into the box of how we 'should' be.

Just notice the feelings of attachment and your reactions and then let it go without too much analysis. You might want to make a change. Do what feels right for you. The important thing is not to change anything because you think you should. You could change or adjust if you want to. Force nothing, just notice it as part of your Mindfulness practice as you move through life on a day-to-day basis. This pausing to just notice can help slow down our reactions which might go from zero to one hundred on a scale of anxiety, shame, anger or any other negative emotion. Besides slowing down these undesired reactions that could lead to many unwanted arguments, recriminations or criticisms, we might become more self-aware and conscious of our values and expectations.

Takeaway:

Attachments are natural and serve many purposes

Attachments can become troublesome when we hang on to them too tightly

By becoming more aware of our attachments and our responses, we can learn much about ourselves.

By putting our attachments into perspective, we can feel calmer and avoid negative feelings of anxiety, fear, anger or resentment.

Mindfulness Activities

Body Scan

Mindfulness meditation on attachment

Be aware of the times in your day when you feel that an idea, opinion, person, place or thing you have an attachment to is challenged.

Record your observations in your journal. Don't be in a rush to change or adjust anything. Just notice and observe.

Notice this with a compassionate attitude.

Don't Wait Until You're Ready.

As promised in the chapter on procrastination, here is an extract from my book "Change Your Life Today" which I hope you find useful.

We all have a little voice in our head. You know the one. It's the voice that tells you that you're wrong, that you are too slow, too fat, too lazy, too dumb, too clever, too young, too old, too tall, too short, too hairy, too bald, too underqualified, too overqualified, too experienced, too inexperienced, and so forth. It's the voice that beats you up when you make a mistake.

Psychologists often call this voice the Inner Critic. It sits in judgment of you all the time. But I think that gives it too much of a sense of authority, which is partly why people get pushed around by this inner voice. They think it's in charge.

I like to think of it as the little voice of your fears. It comes from past pain. It comes from all those times when life has hurt you. It's actually a voice of compassion because it wants you to avoid feeling pain again. It associates change with pain because you have experienced pain in the past when change has randomly been imposed upon you.

So, when you decide you want to make changes, it says, "Whoa, wait a minute. Are you sure about doing that? It would expose you to possible failure, and that hurts. Wouldn't it be better that you carry on doing what you're doing now? You know what that's like. It might not be what you desire, but at least you know what you're going to get."

Sometimes the voice will do a good job and keep you from getting into trouble. But it can also keep you in a situation that you would be best to move on from, because it tries to persuade you to stay with what you have, even if what you have is not what you want.

The voice tells you to stay in the same uninspiring job, stay at the same weight, stay with a partner who is hurting you, keep consuming things you know are bad for you, or stay in the same neighbourhood although you hate it. The voice argues the case for staying with what is familiar, rather than experience something new.

Working with clients, I find one of the biggest difficulties in my job is that I am competing with this voice of their Inner Critic. During the hour that I spend with a client, we can get a lot of things agreed, and the client goes away with a course of action to make positive changes to their life. But once the client leaves the room, the voice of the Inner Critic starts in their head, and it has all week, until the client next sees me, to sow the seeds of self-doubt in the client's mind.

A week is a long time for the voice to do its worst. And that's what the voice likes best, time to work with. So, it will intrude on your thoughts while you are at work, or when you are watching TV. Its favourite trick is to wake you up in the middle of the night and start you worrying.

Clearly, if you want to make changes in your life, you need to get the upper hand on the voice, or it will sabotage your plans every time. Here's how:

Take some action immediately. Don't wait until you think you're ready - that gives the voice time to sabotage you. You will never be 100% ready, anyway. Make a start. You will take the voice by surprise because you will be taking yourself by surprise. And that will give you something very valuable:

Momentum.

And momentum will crush the voice of your fears.

So, if you were planning to study for a new qualification, get online and sign up now. If you intended to start a healthy eating plan on the first day of next month, start now instead, today. Clear out the cupboards of all your junk food and donate it to the food bank.

When I tried to give up smoking in the past, I always tried to start on a date and time I had decided in advance. It never worked. Then one day, at about eight o'clock in the evening, I suddenly decided to stop. It was so sudden, 10 seconds earlier I had no idea I was going to quit. My Inner Critic was completely taken by surprise and kept quiet.

It was one of those random moments in life that I hadn't seen coming. I could have ignored it, and carried on smoking, but I decided to go with it. The following morning, when the cravings started to give me a hard time, my Inner Critic had had time to get over the shock of my sudden action, and it tried to persuade me to smoke. But, by that time, I had already gone 12 hours and I had momentum. I thought: let's get this done. I haven't smoked since, which shows the power of not waiting till you're ready and using randomness in your life to your advantage.

When I wrote my first book, a similar thing happened. At the time, I had been carrying out a lot of counselling work at a hospital out-patient facility with problem drinkers. The results had been excellent and I believed that I had valuable research that I should share with all drinkers in need of support, not just the ones in my town.

I decided to write an article about my work to submit to a magazine. But I quickly realized that I had so much information to share, that I was writing the introduction to a book instead of an article. I decided to carry on and get it done quickly. Three months later, my book "Alcohol and You" was selling on major online platforms, and I was receiving messages from people about how life-changing they had found it.

If I had delayed, if I had thought, "I'll start when I have more time", I would probably never have written the book. The voice of my Inner Critic would have had a chance to plant doubt in my mind. It would have said things like: "Who do you think you are? Are you sure you're qualified enough? Perhaps you should do another five years of research? Why do you think you can write?" And so on.

But because I got on with it immediately, my voice of self-doubt got trampled as I ran down The Path to my goal.

A few years ago, my wife was very unhappy in her job. She was a teacher. She was working ridiculously long hours, had a long commute to her school, she was coming home late, exhausted, with work she still needed to do at home. Her doctor diagnosed her with stress. Something had to change. It would have seemed sensible for her to start applying for other jobs, but it could have taken months to organize a suitable new post. She couldn't wait. Her happiness and health were on the line.

She quit her job, with no other job to go to. At this point, her Inner Critic could have gone crazy, beating her up for doing something so reckless. But it didn't have time, as she took immediate action.

She had always loved animals. Where we lived at the time was in the countryside. Our garden backed onto hundreds of acres of quiet country lanes and fields. She loved nothing more than taking our dog on long walks, as it was perfect dog-walking country. She announced she was going to start a business looking after dogs.

Right away, she started putting out adverts on cheap or free web sites and social media. I designed a small, business web site for her. She bought business insurance. The phone started ringing. She had momentum. Within a few days, she was in business and the dogs started arriving. In her first month, she earned nearly as much as she had been earning as a teacher, doing something she loved.

The important thing to grasp is that change happened on the very first day.

Thank You.

Thank you for reading "Emotions".

If you have found this book helpful, I would be massively grateful if you could find a few moments to post a review on Amazon.

Printed in Great Britain
by Amazon